Astropsychology

A Journey To Yourself

Thaya Edwards

General Disclaimer: This book is provided for information purposes only, with no guarantee of accuracy; it is not intended as a substitute for medical advice, nor as a claim for its effectiveness in treating any symptoms or disease. If symptoms persist, seek professional medical advice; minor symptoms can often be a sign of a more serious underlying condition.

The American Federation of Asrologers does not accept any responsibility for the consequences of any action taken as a result of any of the content of this book, and makes no warranties regarding the value or utility of the information and resources contained in this book.

Copyright 2022 by Thaya Edwards

No part of this book may be reproduced or transcribed in any form or by any means, electronic or mechanical, including photocopying or recording or by any information storage and retrieval system without written permission from the author and publisher, except in the case of brief quotations embodied in critical reviews and articles. Requests and inquiries may be mailed to: American Federation of Astrologers, Inc., 6535 S. Rural Road, Tempe, AZ 85283.

ISBN-978-0-86690-683-8

Cover Design: Celeste Nash-Weninger

Published by:
American Federation of Astrologers, Inc.
6535 S. Rural Road
Tempe, AZ 85283

www.astrologers.com

Contents

Introduction: Where To Look For the True Self?   v

Chapter 1: Subtypes of Zodiac Signs   1

Chapter 2: Natural Elements and Human Temperaments   29

Chapter 3: Planets From the Psychological Point of View   43

Chapter 4: Venus: What Is Love For us?   47

Chapter 5: Moon Phases And Our Wheel Of Reincarnations   55

Chapter 6: Moon in signs – The mirror world of our soul; The distortion of reality and our fears   61

Chapter 7: Mercury – See Who is talking?   73

Chapter 8: Dispositors' Chains And Four Key Planets   81

Chapter 9: Rising planets   107

Chapter 10: A Scout planet   115

Conclusion   121

Bibliography   122

Appendix 1. Ephemeris of Proserpina   123

Introduction
Where to look for the True Self

A lot of people begin studying astrology (and psychology as well) for the main purpose of trying to figure out who they really are. Astrology can definitely help here, although it is no substitute for self-awareness. However, together they can change your life or, at least, the way you see things. So, where to start?

With your Sun sign, of course. Keep in mind, though, that you might end up being a non-typical representative of your sign and that its description may not fit you. Recently, one person told me: "I am an Aquarius. It means I always look for new things". "Well, I thought, it doesn't look like that to me". Actually, this person has several planets in Capricorn and just the Sun in Aquarius, which makes her a completely different character. The main motto here isn't going to be about changes; it would be more like "I like stability".

In Chapter One I describe four subtypes for every Zodiac sign. However, in order to find out which one is for you, you need to read Chapter Two and figure out your main element. Don't be discouraged if you aren't able to do this, should most of your elements be equal. Having balanced elements is an advantage. In this particular case it is recommended to go with the main element of the sign (for example, Air for Gemini or Water for Pisces) or the rising sign.

I found that knowing elements and matching them to temperaments is super-helpful in understanding oneself and others. Elements by themselves explain a lot of differences in our personalities. In relationships, the awareness (and acceptance) of differences can be a crucial point. I consider the second part of Chapter Two even more important because it gives some ideas about ways of making personal changes. It shouldn't be a secret to you (if you are reading this book) that our souls came into this world with certain purposes. One of these purposes is to get better and more advanced on a spiritual level. The Chapter about elements provides glimpses of whether we need to develop particular personal qualities in this lifetime.

Even if you are completely new to astrology, you will still be able to use this book. I included some information about signs and planets glyphs for non-astrologers. If you print your chart from the free astrological software on the Internet, with the help of this book you will be able to read it. To a certain degree, of course...

Since various planets are responsible for different psychological parts, they all need to be studied. Please don't mix them up: Mercury, for example, is responsible only for the mind, not emotional responses. For the latter, look at the Moon's position. The real Art of Astrology is putting all this information together and seeing the whole picture. It can be challenging because the majority of our personalities have many facets. However, it might be pleasant and enlightening to find an explanation of some personal traits. That's where we usually hear: "Ah! That's why!"

Also please refrain from making fast conclusions about other people if you are a beginner in astrology. I heard somebody exclaiming: "I found out that my husband's Mercury is in Pisces. That's why he can't do anything right!" Needless to say, it might not be wise to tell people about your discoveries right away. If we want, we can find explanations (and excuses) for anything (absolutely anything) in a natal chart. However, that isn't the goal of this book. Rather, I am hoping to help readers in understanding their true characters and abilities.

Chapter Five – the Moon phases also has some information about where we stand on our wheel of reincarnations (just a glimpse of it).

Two chapters relate to psychology more than the others: Chapter Six, The Moon in signs – the mirror world of our soul, and Chapter Eight. Dispositors' chains. The chapter about the Moon in signs isn't typical: there is also the description of possible fears and the formation of certain psychological complexes. Please keep in mind that these are just possibilities and you might not have these troubles. However, it is good to be aware since denial has never helped anyone.

Chapter Eight is the most complicated one but it also can be the most helpful for deep, inner work. The chapter about Dispositors' Chains has been written for people who want to figure out the strongest and weakest parts of their character and are willing to work with them. Mastering this Chapter can be super-useful for psychologists.

You can find a lot of useful information about career guidance throughout this book. We all have more than one ability; we just need to find and then develop them. The last chapter, related to a Scout-planet, isn't about career choices only. It is also about our way of self-development. I found it very beneficial for parents to know their child's Scout-planet.

1

Subtypes of Zodiac Signs

People just love to read their horoscopes – even those who say that astrology is nonsense. Sometimes people complain that the description of the sign doesn't really sound like them. There is no surprise there. How is it possible to divide all of mankind into twelve groups and tell them that they are all the same? Although it is true that representatives of one sign have a lot in common, there are always definite differences. I am sure that in your life experience you have known some Pisces who didn't look even remotely similar or a couple of Leos with completely different attitudes, etc.

All of us have unique personalities and the chance of finding two people on this Earth with identical natal charts is remote in the extreme. However, we sometimes like the feeling of belonging as well as wanting explanations for why we are who we are. Astrology offers both of those but with some limitations, particularly where generalization is concerned. In this chapter I'll try to explain to readers who don't know astrology why we can be similar in one way, yet different in many others, when compared to representatives of our Zodiac sign. The explanation is aided by the fact that our signs have subtypes.

You can see the main (classical) element for signs below:

Fire – Aries, Leo, Sagittarius
Earth – Taurus, Virgo, Capricorn
Air – Gemini, Libra, Aquarius
Water – Cancer, Scorpio, Pisces

Those are the main elements that might not work for everyone. In order to personalize the information about signs we can divide every sign into four different categories according to the main element in one's chart. There are four elements: water, fire, air and earth (don't be confused with the Chinese tradition which has five elements). In our chart we can have one or two main elements, meaning we can become a Water Aries, an Earth Scorpio or a Fire Pisces and so on. In order to understand what element dominates your life, you will need your own, personal natal chart. We will learn how to figure out your main element in Chapter Two but for now I'll give the main rules that should be taken into consideration when determining a subtype of the Sun sign. (For non-astrologers: your sign means the Zodiac sign where the Sun was located in the moment of your birth). We need to take into consideration:

- The sign of the Moon
- The strong element determining the subtype (see Chapter Two)
- The planet ruling this subtype if it is strong (mentioned in every subtype's description)
- The rising sign
- The planets of the subtype's element if they are on your Ascendant (knowledge of the exact time of birth is necessary)

Planets Belonging To The Elements

Element	Planets
Fire	Sun, Mars, Jupiter
Water	Moon, Neptune, Pluto
Air	Mercury, Uranus, Chiron
Earth	Venus, Saturn, Proserpina

Those are the main rules. They might seem complicated but they will be explained later when we look at chart examples. Please keep in mind that sometimes there is no pure subtype, as one might be impossible to find when the elements in the chart are in balance (equal).

Aries

Fire Aries.

The ruling planet for this subtype is Mars – which is the general ruler of Aries – and the main element of this sign is Fire.

This is the most aggressive Aries. Everything that has been said about Aries' being super-active, impulsive, a born leader and brave (to the point of recklessness sometimes), can be found here. For them sheer force is the best way of action. They are always ready to take impulsive actions and have no patience. Fire Aries are straight-forward, courageous, optimistic and enthusiastic. We can really see a sign of pioneers in this subtype. In the worst-case scenario, they can be rude, cruel and destructive. If Mercury is also in Aries, representatives of this Zodiac subtype often have a hoarse voice.

There are a lot of politicians and warlords with this Zodiac subtype, as well actors and singers.

Fire Aries celebrities: Tamerlane (with an addition of Water), Ian Smith, Nikita Khrushchev (with a very strong Air), Lady Gaga, Celine Dion, Marlon Brando, Steven Seagal, Omar Sharif (with an addition of Air) and Diana Ross (also with Air).

Sometimes it is easy to figure out a subtype of a sign and sometimes it is not. Below you can see the chart of Ian Smith, the former prime minister (or dictator) of Rhodesia. This is a simple case: a typical Fire Aries. Fire is the dominating element (with six planets in Fire signs), the Moon is in the Fire sign Leo and the Ascendant is in Sagittarius.

Air Aries

As you have figured out, the dominating element is Air. The Sun is the main planet here (the Sun is in exaltation in Aries).

This is a very active and creative Aries but not so aggressive. They

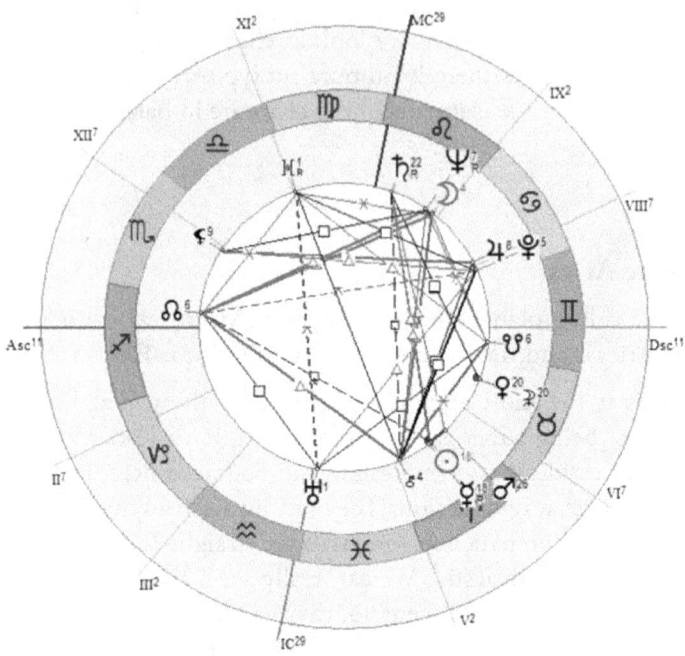

Figure 1: Ian Smith April 8, 1919, 21:00 GMT +2, Selukwe, Zimbabwe

☉ 17 ♈ 53'	♄ 21 ♌ 33' ℞	⚷ 8 ♏ 25'
☽ 3 ♌ 22'	♅ 0 ♓ 21'	⚶ 19 ♉ 53'
☿ 17 ♈ 02' ℞	♆ 6 ♌ 33' ℞	]·[0 ♎ 10' ℞
♀ 19 ♉ 48'	♇ 4 ♋ 38'	⚸ 3 ♈ 47'
♂ 25 ♈ 12'	☊ 05 ♐ 02'	Asc 10 ♐ 55'
♃ 7 ♋ 54'	☋ 05 ♊ 02'	Mc 28 ♌ 51'

are never rude like the first type can be. They are good with contacts, like to show off, pretend to impose royalty and are generally respectful towards others. They have a lot of creative abilities. In the worst-case scenario, they are arrogant and boisterous.

Both Fire and Air Aries' have great strength and stamina. Among the Air subtype we can find a lot of creative people: writers, artists, actors.

Air Aries celebrities: Swami Narayanananda, Sergei Rachmaninoff (with an addition of Fire).

Water Aries

This subtype is related to Pluto.

Water Aries are Aries with possible emotional complexes. They can be gloomy and negative, with difficulties in communicating. Quite often Water Aries' have an increased sexuality which the best of them transforms into creative art. They have a huge inner power which sometimes isn't directed properly and leads them to self-destruction. Their heavy emotions are ready to "explode"; they don't "eat" themselves from the inside like Scorpios do but direct the outbursts outside to other people. This subtype is probably the most difficult of all.

Water Aries celebrities: Vincent Van Gogh (with Fire), Johann Sebastian Bach, Giacomo Casanova, Francisco de Goya, Montserrat Caballe (with an addition of Fire and Earth), Nikolai Gogol (with Air).

As you might notice, it is not that easy to figure out the subtype of Van Gogh's personality. The Water element is definitely very strong but so too is the Fire element. The Moon is in Sagittarius, the Fire sign. Still, I would say that Vincent Van Gogh has the Water subtype (his ASC is in Cancer – Water sign). If you are familiar with his biography, you might agree. He was a very difficult person to be around; not many people could stand being close to him for any length of time. He also had a lot of emotional issues which he tried to cure through his art.

Earth Aries.

The main planet here is Venus (which is in detriment in Aries).

This type is unusually soft for Aries'. They don't look like Aries' at all because instead of active strength this subtype shows gentleness, submissiveness, and a lack of confidence. They are not leaders; on the contrary, they need somebody to lead them. The worst of them look pitiful; the best are very creative in sentimental and sensitive ways. Quite often they are unsatisfied in life and deep inside they are feeling cheated.

Earth Aries celebrities: Mary Tudor, Queen of France; Mstislav

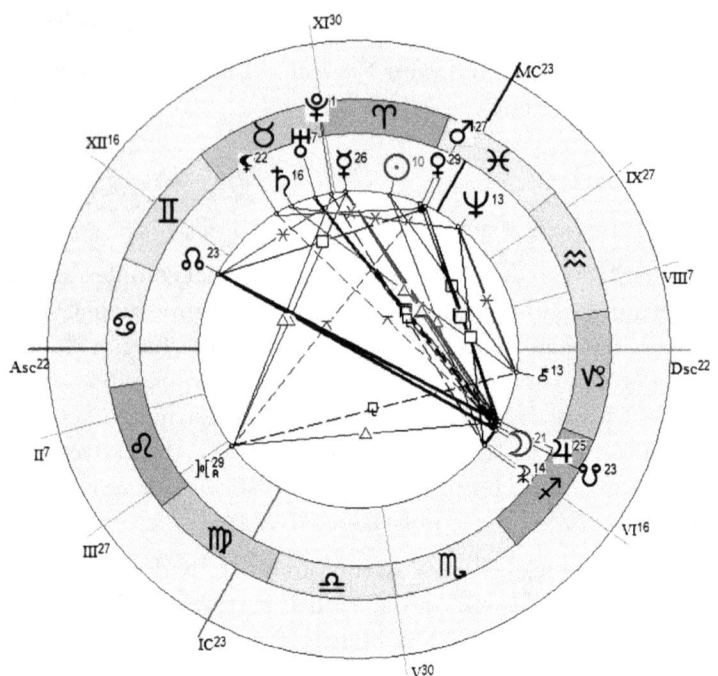

Figure 2: Vincent Van Gogh March 30, 1853, 11:00 am, GMT +0:18:40, Zundert, Netherlands

☉ 9 ♈ 39'	♄ 15 ♉ 57'	☾ 21 ♉ 58'
☽ 20 ♐ 44'	♅ 6 ♉ 48'	♃ 13 ♐ 54'
☿ 25 ♈ 36'	♆ 12 ♓ 13'	]·[28 ♌ 34' ℞
♀ 28 ♓ 03'	♇ 0 ♉ 46'	⚷ 12 ♑ 51'
♂ 26 ♓ 08'	☊ 22 ♊ 28'	Asc 21 ♋ 09'
♃ 24 ♐ 16'	☋ 22 ♐ 28'	Mc 22 ♓ 05'

Rostropovich (with the influence of other elements).

For some people it is impossible to determine their sign subtype because the majority of elements are equal. For example, Charlie Chaplin and Jackie Chan are balanced Aries'. In the future I won't mention people with equal elements. I will say, however, that should you discover that your elements are balanced, there is a reason for you to celebrate.

Taurus

Earth Taurus.

This subtype is related to Venus, the basic Taurus' ruler.

These people are usually calm, soft, and hard-working (although they don't talk much about their accomplishments), patient and persistent. They have good artistic taste but can be slow in developing creative skills and can be perfectionists when it comes to keeping their household. This subtype could also be a slave to passion and material attachment.

Earth Taurus celebrities: Karl Marx, Adolf Hitler (surprise, surprise!), Sigmund Freud, Salvador Dali (with an addition of Fire), George Clooney (not a pure Earth type).

Fire Taurus.

The main planet here is Mars, which is exactly opposite to Venus. So we should expect somebody completely different from the first type… and we would be right.

Taurus is generally not a particularly active sign but the Fire subtype is very dynamic. It is also not patient, unlike the Earth subtype. Fire Taurus' are independent, active, practical, stubborn, jealous and possessive. Usually they are honest and will fight for their principles. They also can be rude and aggressive.

There are a lot of scientists, technicians, and politicians in this subtype.

Fire Taurus celebrities: Che Guevara (with Water), Saddam Hussein, Al Pacino.

Air Taurus.

The main planet is the Moon, which is in exaltation in Taurus.

This subtype is attractive and can definitely use their charm. They are sociable, soft, sensitive and have a sense of humor. However, they are also very practical and can be pretty persistent. Air Taurus likes beauty, comfort, good food, etc. Women can keep their youth and beauty for a long time. There are many dancers, actors and musicians among them.

Air Taurus celebrities: Pope John Paul II (with the Earth addition), William Shakespeare.

Water Taurus.

Pluto has a big influence here and he is in his fall in this sign.

In calm times they may be unnoticeable and unimpressive people, however, when Pluto's time comes (meaning disturbances, extremes), everything changes. It takes a lot of time for them to get ready, but then they become as unstoppable as an avalanche. There are a lot of revolutionary leaders there. This subtype has great difficulty in communicating but needs crowds in order to "be somebody"; then they can become leaders and organizers. They are not so attached to comfort like other Taurus' subtypes and can be very minimalistic.

There are many political leaders, known for slow accumulation of power, in this subtype.

Water Taurus celebrities: Mark Zuckerberg, Audrey Hepburn, Penelope Cruz.

Gemini

Air Gemini.

These are typical Geminis ruled by Mercury, in their own element.

The Air subtype is easy-going, flexible, sociable, active, changeable and adaptable. They also can be shallow, careless, irresponsible, very talkative (mostly talking about nothing) and emotionally cold. It is very easy to be with them but don't look for deep relationships there. They have a talent for languages and are very good as salespeople and the service workers.

Air Gemini celebrities: Queen Victoria, Paul McCartney (with a strong Fire), Henry Kissinger.

Fire Gemini.

The planet for this subtype is Jupiter which is in his detriment in

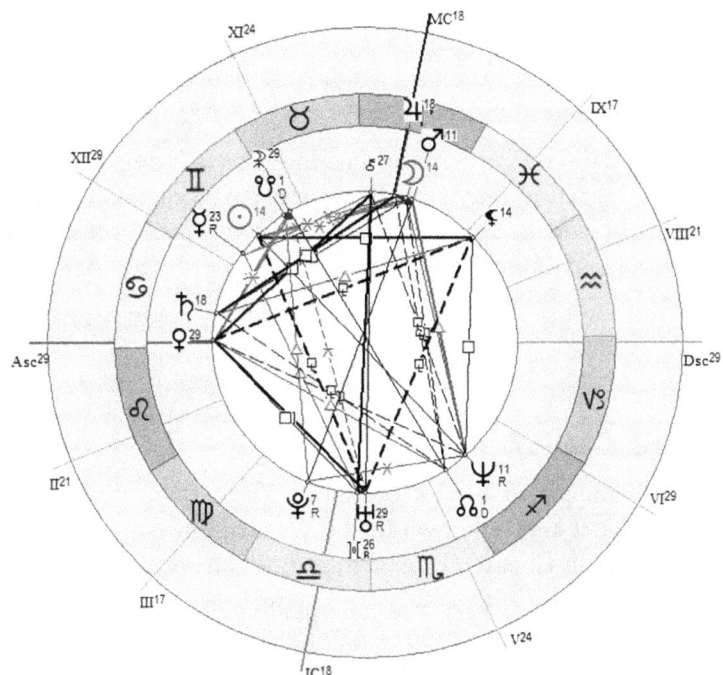
Figure 3: Angelina Jolie June 4, 1975, 9:09 am GMT-7, Los Angeles, CA

☉ 9 ♈ 39'	♄ 15 ♉ 57'	⚷ 21 ♉ 58'
☽ 20 ♐ 44'	♅ 6 ♉ 48'	⚴ 13 ♐ 54'
☿ 25 ♈ 36'	♆ 12 ♓ 13'	]·[28 ♌ 34' ℞
♀ 28 ♓ 03'	♇ 0 ♉ 46'	⚸ 12 ♑ 51'
♂ 26 ♓ 08'	☊ 22 ♊ 28'	Asc 21 ♋ 09'
♃ 24 ♐ 16'	☋ 22 ♐ 28'	Mc 22 ♓ 05'

Gemini.

They have the general Gemini's cheerfulness, mobility and vividness but they are more authoritarian, opinionated and impulsive. The Fire type is still good in contacts; however, they tend to be less polite and

Subtypes of the Zodiac

often put distance between themselves and others. They might appear to be stable – on the surface – but nervousness and restlessness reside within. There are many military people and policemen among them as well as teachers and scientists.

Fire Gemini celebrities: Angelina Jolie, Nicole Kidman, Clint Eastwood, Peter the Great, Dante Alighieri (with Air), Federico Garcia Lorca, Muammar al-Gaddafi, Donald Trump (Air and Water are also there but Earth is completely absent).

If you look at the chart of Angelina Jolie (Figure 3), you can see right away that she is not a typical Gemini. With four planets in Aries, including the Moon and Mars, she could be something else. And she is…

Earth Gemini.

The main planet here is Proserpina. Proserpina is an as-yet undiscovered planet and unknown in the Western astrology. I will explain more about her in Chapter Three. Proserpina is in exaltation in Gemini.

This is not only a very rare subtype, but also the most stable. The Earth element imbues them with good logic and strong common sense. There are always constant inner changes behind their impenetrable, calm appearance. They are observant and astute as well as being possessed of excellent logic, though they can be very attached to material comforts. We can find devoted scientists and philosophers among this type.

Earth Gemini celebrities: John F. Kennedy, Pope Pius XI.

Water Gemini.

Neptune is the main planet for this subtype.

These Geminis are less cheerful, being more of a melancholic temperament. Their mood changes all the time: a swing from melancholy to agitated joy is not uncommon. This subtype is very sensitive, intuitive and easy to influence. A lot in their character and life depends on their environment. Water Geminis can be great psychologists or mediums. They look a little bit like Pisces though without Pisces' depth. They can also be unreliable, immature and out of focus and they can't stand being alone.

Water Gemini celebrities: Marilyn Monroe, Marquis de Sade (with Earth), Igor Stravinsky.

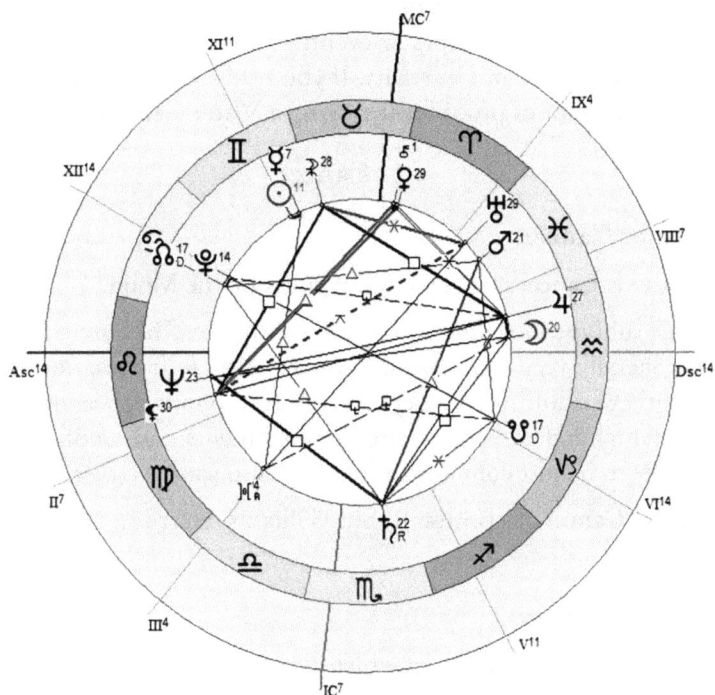

Figure 4: Marilyn Monroe June 1, 1926 9:30 am GMT -8, Los Angeles, CA

☉ 9 ♈ 39'	♄ 15 ♉ 57'	⚷ 21 ♉ 58'
☽ 20 ♐ 44'	♅ 6 ♉ 48'	⚴ 13 ♐ 54'
☿ 25 ♈ 36'	♆ 12 ♓ 13'	].[28 ♌ 34' ℞
♀ 28 ♓ 03'	♇ 0 ♉ 46'	⚵ 12 ♑ 51'
♂ 26 ♓ 08'	☊ 22 ♊ 28'	Asc 21 ♋ 09'
♃ 24 ♐ 16'	☋ 22 ♐ 28'	Mc 22 ♓ 05'

It is difficult to figure out the Zodiac subtype for Marilyn Monroe (Figure 4): Air, Water and Fire are prominent elements. The main reason why she is more of the Water type is because Neptune, belonging to the Water element, was rising at the moment of her birth (is located on the

Ascendant). Neptune makes a person very sensitive, sometimes idealistic and easily infatuated by people or events. Sometimes these people tend to live in their dreams, not in reality. If you read a biography of Marilyn, you might find a lot of proof for her being a Water Gemini.

Cancer

Water Cancer.

Water is Cancer's element and is ruled by the Moon.

This subtype looks inert, soft and dreamlike. They are emotional, passive, generally very adaptable and prefer to be followers, not leaders. However, there is a firm core beyond this amorphous appearance. They are sentimental and capable of strong attachments and sacrifice. Water Cancers like to be just contemplators. They also can be clever "users".

Water Cancer celebrities: Robin Williams, Harrison Ford, Camille Pissarro.

Earth Cancer.

The main planet is Saturn which is in his detriment in Cancer.

This type can be compared to the hermit crab, which always carries his shell with him where he hides in order not to show his vulnerability. They can play a tough and strong personality and can be critical, gloomy and sarcastic. They often have a heavy burden of memories and find it difficult to let go of the past. They are rarely talkative or sociable, mostly keeping their distance. Earth types like to get to the core of things – including their own character. They could be great psychologists if not for their lack of sociability. They also can be pessimistic, secretive and suspicious.

Earth Cancer celebrities: 14th Dalai Lama (with an addition of Water), Ernest Hemingway.

Fire Cancer.

Jupiter, exalting in Cancer, is the main figure here.

They are active and social, which is not a known trait for other Cancers. In addition to being optimistic and generous, this subtype is very authoritarian as well. They like traditions and try to teach them.

Generally they are good teachers as well as actors and military people. As with all Cancers, they are emotional, very touchy and intuitive. Usually they are very attached to their loved ones but can also have several partners during lifetime. They like to show off.

Fire Cancer celebrities: Nelson Mandela (with Water), Tom Cruise, Tom Hanks, Henry VIII of England, Gina Lollobrigida.

Air Cancer.

The main planet is Mars, which is in his fall here.

This type is uncontrollable, sly, capricious, sensitive, and can be hysterical. They are good at socializing, and are usually charming, though it is just a façade. They like to play the role of a powerful person. They are unpredictable and though usually not brave, they are able to show courage when given over to emotional outbursts. This is an active type.

We can find a lot of media people, writers, travelers, servers, hairdressers and waiters among this subtype.

Air Cancer celebrities: George W. Bush (with Fire), Franz Kafka (with Earth), Edgar Degas.

Leo

Fire Leo.

It is natural to be "on fire" for Leos. Fire Leos are the authentic Leos. The Sun is their ruler.

They are optimistic, very creative, generous and proud and have noble manners and esthetic tastes.

They open their hearts to those people who demonstrate an appreciation for them but are distant and cold towards all others. In the worst-case scenario, they are self-centered, vain and unnatural. They tend to be megalomaniacs who, when all is said and done, really don't care about other people.

Fire Leo celebrities: Louis Armstrong, Whitney Houston, Antonio Banderas, Jacqueline Kennedy-Onassis, Halle Berry.

Water Leo.

The main planet is Pluto, which is exalted in this sign.

Water Leos are powerful with great physical strength. They act like lions: appearing a bit sleepy or relaxed one moment, then suddenly transforming and jumping into action. They can achieve a lot with one spurt. There is an almost magical influence on people from this type. They don't put up with lying and don't forgive insults. Water Leo is dreadful in his anger and very generous in his mercy. They are very ambitious. In the worst-case scenario this subtype can be pretty destructive.

Water Leo celebrities: Mata Hari (with Fire), Coco Chanel, Robert de Niro (with Earth).

Air Leo.

Uranus is ruling this type and he is in his detriment here.

They are generally joyful, like to have fun and tend to be very adventurous. Air Leos are extremely creative, always seeming able to come up with a lot of new ideas. They like to play (in love as well) and they are passionate about that which they undertake but they can't stand any limitation on their personal freedom. This subtype includes scientists who are ahead of their time.

Air Leo celebrities: Barack Obama (with Fire), Helena Blavatsky, Henry Ford, Bill Clinton, Sandra Bullock, Benito Mussolini.

This is a pretty impressive list. Some of those people definitely like/liked to play (Bill Clinton, for example). Others did not... have a look at Barack Obama's chart (Figure 5). His Fire element is strong but Air is also prominent: the Moon in Gemini and Ascendant in Aquarius. However, his air element isn't as strong as Clinton's with five planets and Ascendant in Libra. (Figure 9) Obama isn't "playful" like Clinton also because of his Venus being in Cancer (Bill's Venus is in Libra) which instills more responsibility.

Earth Leo.

Saturn is the main planet here and he is in his detriment in Leo.

This is the most modest type amongst Leos but they can still be very touchy if people don't notice them. They are responsible, persistent, exigent and tough. This type is the least optimistic and cheerful of all Leos, and sometimes seems to completely lack a sense of humor. It might be difficult to be around them because Earth Leos can be gloomy, over-

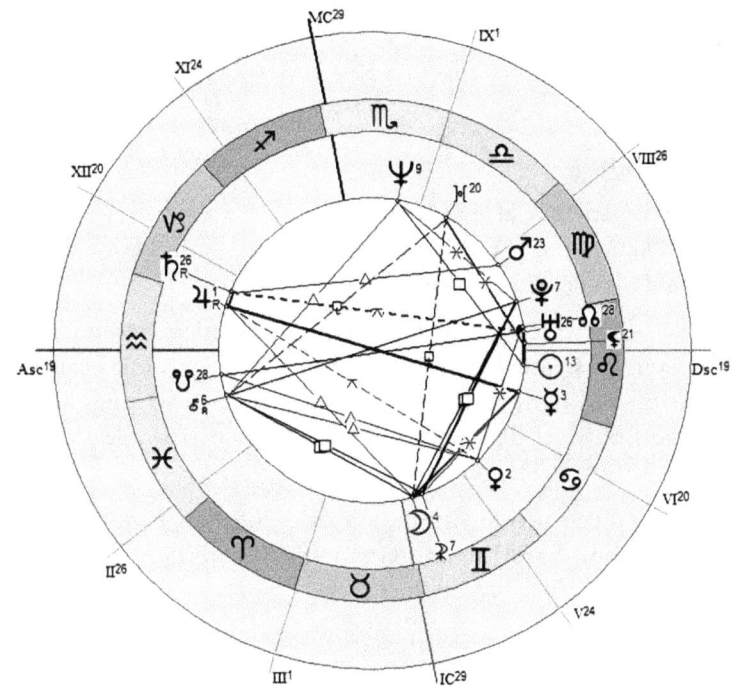

Figure 5: Barack Obama August 4, 1961, 19:24, GMT -10, Honolulu, HI

☉ 12° ♌ 32'	♄ 25° ♑ 19' ℞	⚷ 20° ♌ 34'
☽ 3° ♊ 21"	♅ 25° ♌ 16'	♆ 6° ♊ 59'
☿ 2° ♌ 19'	♆ 8° ♏ 36'	]•[19° ♎ 09'
♀ 1° ♋ 47'	♇ 6° ♍ 58'	⚸ 5° ♓ 19' ℞
♂ 22° ♍ 34'	☊ 27° ♌ 18'	Asc 18° ♒ 03'
♃ 0° ♒ 51' ℞	☋ 27° ♒ 18'	Mc 28° ♏ 54'

critical and always complaining. However, they can also be very successful in life because they are both ambitious and serious and put a lot of passion into achieving their goals.

Subtypes of the Zodiac 23

Earth Leo celebrities: Napoleon I, Madonna, Robert Redford, Dustin Hoffman.

Virgo

Air Virgo.

Virgo is generally an Earth sign but its Air subtype – which is also ruled by Mercury, the general ruler of the sign – took a lot from this planet whose main element is Air.

These Virgos are very sociable, logical, practical, resourceful and witty. Their mind is usually cold and calculating. Air Virgos can be pedantic, critical and boring. They can be very good in writing. There are a lot of scientists, journalists, tour guides and businesspeople among this type.

Air Virgo celebrities: Agatha Christie, Stephen King (with Fire), Sophia Loren (with Earth), David Copperfield (with Fire).

Fire Virgo.

The main planet is Jupiter (in detriment).

Fire Virgos can have a profusely increased sense of duty. They are very demanding towards themselves and others, fastidious and always obedient to authority. They are attached to their family and take good care of their kids (with a lot of demands at the same time). They like to study. In the worst-case scenario, this type can be a horrible bureaucrat and toady to supervisors. No good as a boss.

Fire Virgo celebrities: Louis XIV of France, Freddie Mercury, Paulo Coelho.

Water Virgo.

Venus is the main planet here, and she is in her fall in Virgo.

This subtype can be unbelievably "sweet", but usually this "sweetness" is superficial, fake. However, they can be very charming, trustworthy and attractive; their cold, logical and calculating nature is hidden. They might look at love as a variety of sport and they are very good when it comes to flirting. Water Virgos pay a lot of attention to detail (as do a majority of Virgos) and take good care of their health. Material blessings mean a lot to them.

Water Virgo celebrities: Keanu Reeves (with Earth), Ingrid Bergman (with Fire).

Earth Virgo.

The main planet for this type is Proserpina, which rules Virgo in addition to Mercury. (The significance of Proserpina will be discussed in Chapter Three).

This is a rare subtype of ascetic Virgos. They can comprehend abstract ideas and have a thirst for pure knowledge. Earth Virgos are very responsible and have a huge sense of duty. They are generally modest and don't want much for themselves but can be demanding of themselves and towards others. They are good in planning their life and this is the only subtype which can not only analyze well but is also good in synthesis.

Earth Virgos celebrities: Mere Teresa, Leo Tolstoy, Andrea Bocelli, Dmitry Medvedev, Greta Garbo, Cameron Diaz.

Libra

Water Libra.

This subtype is ruled by Venus, the natural ruler of Libra.

This is a soft, esthetic type with fine manners and a strong dislike for conflicts. They always appreciate beauty and follow the latest fashion trends. They prefer the "golden middle" in everything. Water Libras are sensitive but their feelings are not always deep. Sometimes the appearance is more important for them than the true essence. They are too easy-going for compromises and can be lazy, insincere and dependent. There are many actors, artists and top models among this type.

Water Libra celebrities: Mahatma Gandhi, Deepak Chopra, Aleister Crowley, Jean-Claude Van Damme (with Earth).

Fire Libra.

The main planet is quite unusual for Libra: Mars (in detriment).

This is the most impulsive, passionate and tough type of Libra. They can be loud but not confident at the same time and can go from crazy activity to hesitation, always having doubts. Even if they can fight, they always want to embrace peace and balance. Fire subtype is generally ready to defend justice. The best of them are able to be good politicians.

Fire Libra celebrities: Margaret Thatcher (with Air), Friedrich Nietzsche, Heinrich Himmler.

Earth Libra.

Saturn in exhalation is important for this type.

This subtype is very sensible, with a cold and calculating mind. They, more than other types, are attached to the concept of "elite" and feel the need to observe etiquette. Earth Libras are judgmental (not like other types): they make appraisals and pin a label on people. They have good manners but also can be arrogant. They will listen to other people but will always follow their own opinion. The best of them are fair, respectful and balanced. We can find philosophers, lawyers and writers among this type.

Earth Libra celebrities: Frances of Assisi, John Lennon (with Air), Catherine Zeta-Jones (with Air).

Air Libra.

As you might know, Air is the primary Libra element. This subtype is ruled by Chiron.

They can get along with people better than anyone else. Though very sociable, they also like the "elitist society". They use diplomacy a lot and make good peacemakers, arbitrators, diplomats and judges. Air type is probably ready for compromises more than others; they might exhibit paradoxical behavior, being unpredictable and unreliable. They can be successful businessmen because of their excellent social and organization skills. The worst of them are insincere and shallow.

Air Libra celebrities: Vladimir Putin, Brigitte Bardot, F. Scott Fitzgerald, Viggo Mortensen, Sting, Kate Winslet.

Scorpio

Fire Scorpio.

The main planet here is Mars, one of the natural rulers of Scorpios.

This is a tough, passionate and honest Scorpio. It might be difficult to be around them because they are very demanding; however, if they like you, they can give a lot. This type is reserved, not that good at socializing, practical, hard-working and generally gloomy. At the same time they are very loyal and devoted to their close people. Usually they don't like themselves.

Fire Scorpio celebrities: Bill Gates, Indira Gandhi (with the strong Earth), Voltaire (with Air), Fyodor Dostoyevsky (with Earth).

Water Scorpio.

Pluto is the ruler here.

Water Scorpios are leaders in extreme situations. They are absolutely fearless and thrive on risk. When life is normal and comfortable, they are bored and will try to find adventure. What others consider chaos is their harmony. They have amazing survival skills and great influence on people. Living with a Water Scorpio might be difficult because it's like always waiting for a volcanic eruption. In the worst-case scenario they can be revengeful, spiteful and aggressive.

Water Scorpio celebrities: Leonardo DiCaprio (with Air), Condoleezza Rice, Jodie Foster (with Earth), Grace Kelly, Hillary Clinton, Diego Maradona, Meg Ryan, Sathya Sai Baba.

Earth Scorpio.

The main planet is Venus which is in detriment in this sign.

This is the most sexual type: very attractive, even mesmerizing. Women in this subtype can project an image of a "femme fatale". Earth Scorpios very rarely get into conflicts; they are not risky like other types. Earth subtype is usually very possessive and jealous. In the beginning they can be charming but then will make everyone serve them. In the best-case scenario, this is a very creative subtype.

Earth Scorpio celebrities: Pablo Picasso, Julia Roberts, Robert F. Kennedy.

Air Scorpio.

The main planet is Uranus which is in exaltation in Scorpio.

This is a very rare subtype. They are unpredictable, passionate and proud and, though they can communicate with anyone, they tend always to keep their distance. Very often Air Scorpios are lonely and people frequently think them strange and arrogant (which they are not). They have great intuition and usually are open-minded. The best of them can overcome Scorpio's passions.

Air Scorpio celebrities: Jawaharlal Nehru, Francois Mitterrand, Ivanka Trump.

Sagittarius

Fire Sagittarius.

Here we can see the real Jupiter, or Zeus.

This subtype is very energetic, enthusiastic, authoritarian and impulsive. Fire Sagittarius' have excellent organization skills, enjoy variety and don't avoid responsibility. They are usually conservative and very ambitious and are never satisfied with what they have, always wanting more. In the worst-case scenario, Fire subtype can be too bossy, intolerant and arrogant and prone to showing off. There are a lot of politicians, priests, teachers and travelers amongst them.

Fire Sagittarius celebrities: Ludwig van Beethoven (with Earth), Winston Churchill, Jimi Hendrix (with Water), Jacques Chirac, Mark Twain, Tina Turner, Britney Spears (with Air).

Earth Sagittarius.

Mercury in detriment is the main planet.

This subtype is extremely practical with a developed common sense and rational mind. They are enthusiastic and optimistic as well as authoritarian – like the majority of Sagittarius'. Earth subtypes have great communication skills but their organization skills are frequently lacking. They are pretty observant and have a strong system of values. There are lots of scientists, inventors, businessmen, writers and athletes within this type. They always take good care of their health and fitness. In the worst-case scenario, this type can be unreliable, unrealistic and greedy.

Earth Sagittarius celebrities: Brad Pitt, Patricia Kaas, Ozzy Osbourne, Joseph Stalin (with Air).

When you look at the chart of Brad Pitt, it is obvious that he be-

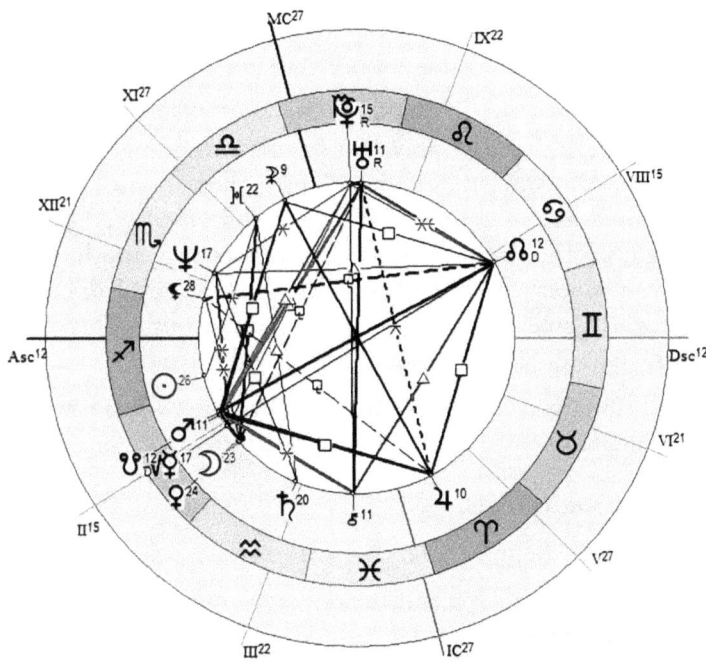

Figure 6: Brad Pitt December 18, 1963, 6:31 am, GMT -6, Shawnee, OK

☉ 25° ♐ 51'	♄ 19° ♒ 08'	⚷ 27° ♏ 03'
☽ 22° ♑ 49'	♅ 10° ♍ 04' ℞	♃ 8° ♎ 50'
☿ 16° ♑ 06'	♆ 16° ♏ 48'	]·[21° ♎ 28'
♀ 23° ♑ 28'	♇ 14° ♍ 13' ℞	⚸ 10° ♓ 34'
♂ 10° ♑ 01'	☊ 11° ♋ 09'	Asc 11° ♐ 54'
♃ 9° ♈ 50'	☋ 11° ♑ 09'	Mc 26° ♍ 58'

longs to the Earth type. He has six planets in the Earth signs (Capricorn and Virgo), including the Moon. There is more of Capricorn in him than Sagittarius.

Subtypes of the Zodiac

Air Sagittarius.

There is a big influence from Chiron – which is in exaltation – in this sign. Chiron in mythology was a centaur, which is the symbol for Sagittarius.

This subtype has an ambivalent nature and often goes to extremes. One day they are students of some "guru" they admire, but the next day this "guru" has no authority anymore, and off they go in search of something else. They need freedom, constant change and lots of travel. They are very mobile and friendly but can also be disloyal and unreliable. Air Sagittarius' can easily lead two lives simultaneously. There are many geologists, archaeologists and doctors among this type.

Air Sagittarius celebrities: Andrew Carnegie (with strong Fire and Water), Francisco Franco, Henri Toulouse-Lautrec.

Water Sagittarius.

Neptune is the ruler here.

This is a rare subtype and the only type of Sagittarius that is very sensitive. Other subtypes have a stronger nervous system. Water Sagittarius' are big idealists who try to understand the meaning of life and believe in a better future. We can find many religious teachers here. They try to live according to their higher principles and suffer when faced with reality. In fact, they are always unhappy with reality. There are also lots of poets in this subtype. The best of Water Sagittarius' are unselfish and capable of an unconditional love. The worst of them are very emotionally unstable, intolerant, always complaining and even fanatical.

Water Sagittarius celebrities: Bruce Lee, Frank Sinatra, Steven Spielberg (with Fire), Uri Geller, Gianni Versace.

Capricorn

Earth Capricorn.

Earth is a natural element for Capricorn and Saturn is its natural ruler.

The Earth subtype is very goal-oriented, persistent, stable, pedantic and sober-minded. They have perfect memory, an effective learning system and demonstrate consistency in everything. However, they might be fixed on the past. Usually they don't talk much and often are loners. This is a demanding but at the same time ascetic type. They never complain but instead can go into deep, quiet depression. This is a very reliable type. It is not possible to influence them. The worst are cold and revengeful. Earth Capricorns can be very patient and usually become successful later in life.

Earth Capricorn celebrities: Aristotle Onassis, Anthony Hopkins, Lara Fabian (with Air), Gerard Depardieu, Nicolas Cage (with Air).

Water Capricorn.

The main planet is the Moon which is in detriment here.

They are steadfast and goal-oriented, like other Capricorn types, but also are sensitive, vulnerable and idealistic. Despite their idealism and daydreaming, when it comes to real-life matters, they become very practical. This subtype is probably the softest of Capricorns. There are a lot of religious people among this type as well as poets, musicians and actors. They can be very patient and have excellent intuition. However, because of their increased sensitivity, accompanied by a reserve nature, they might have numerous emotional complexes.

Water Capricorn celebrities: Martin Luther King, Isaac Newton, Nostradamus, Edgar Allan Poe.

Fire Capricorn.

Mars is ahead of everyone here because he is in exaltation in Capricorn.

In this type we see an impressive force combined with great tenacity. Fire Capricorns are dynamic, brave, persistent, patient and hardworking. Nothing can stop them. They also can be cruel despots who never forgive weakness but respect power.

Fire Capricorn celebrities: Mao Zedong (with a strong Earth), David Bowie, Al Capone, Kevin Costner.

Air Capricorn.

The main planet is Uranus.

The most sociable type of all Capricorns, this is actually a rare subtype. They can be very unpredictable and mutable but also have Capricorn's persistence and stubbornness. Their mind is cool, creative and inventive. They are always in the center of events and can be very spiritual. There are a lot of inventors, scientists and spiritual leaders among this type.

Air Capricorn celebrities: Joan of Arc (with Earth), Swami Vivekananda, Janis Joplin (with Water), Muhammad Ali (with Earth).

Aquarius

Earth Aquarius.

Saturn, one of two natural Aquarius' rulers, is the main planet for this subtype.

Earth Aquarius' always keep their distance, although they can be excellent communicators. They have few close friends but a lot of acquaintances. They value their freedom more than anything else, which explains why they are often alone. They can appear prudish, formal and extremely rational but can go from conservatism to adventurism and back. This subtype can be gloomy and pessimistic. There are philosophers and psychologists among this type.

Earth Aquarius celebrities: Franklin D. Roosevelt (with Air), Ronald Reagan, Grigori Rasputin, Paul Newman (with Water), Nastassja Kinski.

Air Aquarius.

Uranus, the other Aquarius' ruler, is governing here.

This is a very independent and unpredictable subtype. They always live in the future and often are ahead of their time. Planning is not an option for this type. They like to play in life and can fall in love at first sight. Air Aquarius is extremely friendly, witty and sometimes eccentric and like to project a bohemian impression. They really don't care about other people's opinions. In the worst-case scenario, they can be unreliable and very talkative. There are a lot of inventors, journalists, writers, actors and reformers among this type.

Air Aquarius celebrities: Wolfgang Amadeus Mozart (with Fire), Oprah Winfrey, Thomas Edison (with Fire), Omraam Mikhael Aivanhov, Paris Hilton (with Fire).

Fire Aquarius.

The Sun, which is in detriment in this sign, plays an important role for this subtype.

This is a rare type. Fire Aquarius' may seem very modest but there are passions under the surface. This is a very creative type. They always have their own opinion but don't impose it on others. Sometimes they are informal leaders; even they don't have an inclination to leadership and can play the role of "unrecognized genius". The worst of them are selfish, egocentric, unreliable and double-faced.

Fire Aquarius celebrities: Charles Dickens, Nicolas Sarkozy.

Water Aquarius.

Here we have the influence of Neptune.

This is also a very rare subtype. Water Aquarius' are sensitive, idealistic, creative and honest, combining strong faith with a love of freedom. When they are inspired, they can create masterpieces. They are not nearly as sociable as other Aquarius', though they are capable of unconditional love, becoming much attached to their loved ones. Also, they have great intuition and spiritual strength. They can be too passive sometimes and also look like big kids.

Water Aquarius celebrities: Abraham Lincoln (with Fire), Sri Ramakrishna Paramahamsa, Charles Darwin (with Fire), Lord Byron (with Air), John Travolta.

Pisces

Fire Pisces.

Jupiter, one of the natural Pisces' rulers, plays a big role for this subtype.

Fire Pisces' are optimistic, energetic, charming, adaptable and sociable. This is the strongest subtype of Pisces. They are very ambitious and make good managers. They possess excellent organization skills and know how to maneuver, often going for compromises. However, they can be effective leaders only in quiet times. Usually they are good family people. They often have their own secret agenda. We can find many teachers, religious and ideological leaders among this type.

Fire Pisces celebrities: Albert Einstein, Nicolas Copernicus, Mikhail Gorbachev, Antonio Vivaldi (with Air), Ivana Trump (with Air).

Water Pisces.

The second Pisces ruler, Neptune, is more important here.

This subtype is very sensitive, delicate, dependent and easily influenced. They prefer dreaming to action and sometimes lose track of reality. This is a deep type which often lives in its own spiritual world and finds it very difficult to live in a disharmonious environment. The best of them are mystics, psychics, poets and musicians. The worst are deceptive, extremely passive and melancholic.

Water Pisces celebrities: Michelangelo, Galileo Galilei, Elizabeth Taylor (with Fire), Kurt Cobain, Sharon Stone (with Fire), Liza Minnelli, Drew Barrymore, Osama bin Laden.

Air Pisces.

Mercury (in his detriment and fall) is the main planet here.

This is the most cunning Fish ("flying fish"). They are extremely sociable, talkative and friendly (other Pisces tend not to talk much). Their logical mind and intuition are in harmony and they can be quite practical and very good at making a living. Among this type we can find poets, writers, musicians and scientists. In the worst-case scenario, they are artful intrigues who always play at life.

Air Pisces celebrities: Eva Mendes, Jon bon Jovi, Bruce Willis (with Water), Ornella Muti, Justin Bieber (with Water).

Earth Pisces.

Venus in exaltation has great importance here.

This is probably the most beautiful type of Pisces: sensual, soft, sexy and – sometimes – mysterious. They can't imagine their life without love and are capable of very deep feelings. Earth Pisces' love beauty, nature and art. They are polite, charming and delicate and have excellent artistic taste, which is why they can be trendsetters in fashion. They also have very good intuition (as do most Pisces'). There are a lot of psychics, dancers, poets, psychologists and actors among this type. The worst of them can be overly attached to material comforts, spoilt, capricious and inclined to live on somebody else's expense.

Earth Pisces celebrities: Peter Fonda (with Fire), Anna Magnani (with Water).

2

Natural Elements and Human Temperaments

If you are ready for more after reading about your Zodiac subtype, in this chapter we will unfold more mysteries related to four elements (not to be confused with the five Chinese elements). We will also learn how to find a dominating element in our charts. At the end of this chapter you will find information about the qualities of a certain element you have to develop in order to be successful in life.

Main four elements: Fire, Water, Air and Earth, can be found everywhere in nature as well as in human bodies and characters. Since ancient times human temperaments were divided into four groups: choleric, sanguine, phlegmatic and melancholic. Modern psychologists still use this concept. There is a direct correlation between these elements and temperaments. Let's look at them more closely.

Fire Element

People with a distinctive Fire element in their charts have a choleric temperament. The main words for them are action, achievements, energy and leadership.

Fire people have a lot of ambition, energy and drive, and can dominate others (especially if others are of different temperaments). They are courageous, impulsive, creative, confident and sometimes reckless. A choleric person doesn't have any patience; he/she wants everything right now. They have good organization skills, persistence and enthusiasm, along with willfulness, a tendency toward non-compliance and a lack of diplomacy. Fire people can be charismatic leaders. They much prefer to lead than to follow.

They are people of a spurt, an impulse. They want fast realization of their ideas and put a lot of energy into achieving them. However, if success doesn't come quickly, they might lose interest in the project and switch to something else. The negative sides of a choleric can be a hot temper, anger (which doesn't last long, though) and intolerance.

Air Element

Air people have a sanguine temperament. The main things for them are contacts, ideas and energy exchange. The Air element likes to be free and independent.

The main features about the sanguine temperament: it gives a person an easy-going nature, flexibility, general cheerfulness and adaptability. Air people are open-minded, digest information quickly and transfer it to other people. They are extremely sociable and can talk to anyone about anything. They are also active, although in a different way than Fire people. While the latter have a passion inside themselves to go and do things they want, Air people need an outside "push" for action. Sanguines have problems with concentration and can easily change their direction. That's why sometimes they are considered unreliable. Their point of view can be superficial.

Air people are generally very popular because of their optimism and social skills. Their ideal place is in the center of events. We can find a lot of successful journalists among this group. Monotony, routine and boredom are their worst enemies. It is easy to influence an Air person, and often this person won't be able to see if the influence is good or bad: they are too easily carried away and might not have depth required for fair judgment.

Earth Element

Earth people have a phlegmatic temperament. The main traits for them are stability, patience and a practical mind.

A phlegmatic person is usually calm, unemotional, consistent, rational and persistent. Earth people like to see results; they are very persistent in their actions. Their practical mind and excellent common sense serve them well. Phlegmatic is the only temperament that can do a monotonous job. They don't like changes and usually follow a well-known path. Earth people prefer stability and temperance to adventures.

They usually have "golden hands" and are very good with any trades. They also can be excellent accountants, financiers and businesspeople. Their patience is amazing, and they are very reliable people.

The worst of Earth people can be greedy, closed-minded, inert and overly calculating.

Water Element

Water people have a melancholic temperament. They have a much weaker nervous system than other temperaments. The main reason for this is that they are very sensitive. Water element represents feelings and emotions. Water is deep, changeable, flowing and mysterious.

For melancholics their inner world is much more important that the outer one. Their emotions are deep but usually they avoid showing them. Water people are compassionate, receptive and intuitive. They have an amazing imagination and creative abilities. There are many psychologists as well as poets, artists and musicians among them. Their feelings often overpower their rational mind. Water people's moods can change quickly and sometimes other people can't understand why it happened (no visible reasons). The reason for this is the melancholic's sensitivity. Water people, more than other temperaments, need their "other half". They are very attached to their loved ones.

In the worst-case scenario, they can be passive, dependent, lazy, easily depressed and unrealistic.

Water is the most changeable and diverse element. In our world it exists in three shapes: liquid, dense (ice) and gas (steam). That's why representatives of Water signs can be so different from each other. It is especially important for these signs to figure out the certain subtype of the sign because they can be very different.

Some of you, who have read about temperaments before, can point out that there are contradictions between my ideas and the information in some other books. It concerns the statement that Water is in correlation with a melancholic temperament and Earth with phlegmatic. From ancient times some philosophers and psychologists believed that Water is related to a phlegmatic temperament (humor) and Earth to melancholic. I disagree with this statement. I was taught in a different way and my decades of experience and research have confirmed these teachings.

You will come to the same logical conclusion if you think about the essence of the different temperaments. A phlegmatic temperament is very stable and calm, so it definitely belongs to the Earth, not Water, which is so changeable, sensitive and deeply troubled (which is a melancholic, of course).

Now I'd like to encourage you to look at the elements in your chart. In case you are not familiar with astrology, I'll give you the list of signs' glyphs and planetary symbols. You can find free software online for printing your chart and then use the information shown below for the orientation in your horoscope.

♈ Aries	♌ Leo	♐ Sagittarius
♉ Taurus	♍ Virgo	♑ Capricorn
♊ Gemini	♎ Libra	♒ Aquarius
♋ Cancer	♏ Scorpio	♓ Pisces

In order to be sure which element or elements are dominating in your chart you'll have to do a simple calculation. Don't worry, it isn't difficult: the majority of my non-astrological students have been able to do this.

☉ Sun	☽ Moon	☊ North Node
☿ Mercury	♀ Venus	☋ South Node
♂ Mars	♃ Jupiter	⚸ Black Moon Lilith
♄ Saturn	♅ Uranus	⚴ White Moon Selena
♆ Neptune	♇ Pluto	
⚷ Chiron	⯚ Proserpina	

First you need to know which signs belong to which elements.

Fire – Aries, Leo, Sagittarius

Air – Gemini, Libra, Aquarius

Earth – Taurus, Virgo, Capricorn

Water – Cancer, Scorpio, Pisces

Because we want to be confident of the results, I'll give you the points for each planet.

Sun, Moon - 2 points

Mercury, Venus, Mars - 1.5 points

Jupiter, Saturn, Uranus, Neptune, Pluto, Chiron, Proserpina - 1 point

Moon Nodes, Black Moon (Lillith), White Moon (Selena) - .5 point

Don't be surprised that the points are different: personal planets are definitely more important than transpersonal. Now we will be counting the points. Proserpina, Lilith and Selena can be easily omitted. Look at your astrological chart and find planets located in the Fire signs. Then count the points. In order to make life easier, we will use an example. Please look at Figure Two in Chapter One. As an example we'll use the chart of Vincent van Gogh.

The artist, who after his death, has been universally recognized, had a lot of planets in the Fire signs: the Sun and Mercury in Aries, the Moon, Jupiter, South Moon Node and Selena in Sagittarius, and Proserpina in Leo. If we count the points we will get: 2+1.5+2+1+0.5+0.5+1 = 8.5 (for Fire).

Air: North Moon Node in Gemini. That's all: 0.5 points.

Earth: Pluto, Uranus, Saturn and Lilith in Taurus, and Chiron in Capricorn: 1+1+1+0.5+1 = 4.5.

Water: Venus, Mars and Neptune in Pisces: 1.5+1.5+1 = 4.

Fire was a dominating element for Van Gogh, Earth and Water have almost the same number of points and there is almost no Air. I think that Water is still more prominent in his chart than Earth, because both the ASC and MC are in the Water signs. Fire, as the main element, made Vincent van Gogh choleric: very creative, passionate, impatient, hot-tempered and incapable of doing a monotonous job. Water element added some melancholic temperament as well, which "helped" him to be easily depressed. The artist had no Air in his chart which speaks to a considerable lack of communication skills. If you get more information on his life, you will see that communicating properly with people (especially strangers) was a huge challenge for him.

When you count all your points you will be able to see a general portrait of your personality: where you have a lot of something and where something is missing. We were born with these qualities. However, that doesn't mean that they should remain unchanged throughout our lives. The question of whether or not we should change that with which we were born will be discussed later.

If Proserpina, Lilith and Selena are not present in the chart you printed, you can easily go without them.

What kind of temperament would you prefer to have? People of what element would you like to have around you? Is one temperament better than the other? Well, it depends…

Let's look at a possible real-life example. You and your partner need to paint your house. If your partner is a Fire person, a choleric, what might you expect? He\she will be very enthusiastic: this is a big project! He (let's stay with a "he") will start organizing things quickly, and it is better if you are not in his way (he will quickly organize you as well!). A Fire person wants everything to be perfect, in the way he imagined. If it goes wrong, he will become angry. If there is a lack of skills from his side, he will never admit it. The previous enthusiasm will fade away as the day progresses and he begins to see that this project can't be finished fast. A choleric hates monotonous work.

If your partner is an Air person, a sanguine, he will be also enthusiastic in the beginning. While doing something useful, he will also like to have some fun. He will be well prepared for the project: with a few cold beers in the cooler and some nice music. As the day progresses and empty beer cans pile up, your partner will pay less attention to the quality of his work. When a neighbor comes by, they will have a long chat. Then he will leave for a minute to look at the neighbor's car. A minute will become an hour…

You might consider yourself lucky if you have a phlegmatic (an Earth person) as a helper. He won't be tired emotionally and will do the work methodically and with good quality. But he will take his time…

If your partner is a Water person, a melancholic, he might be almost as good as a phlegmatic; however, a melancholic isn't equipped for the monotonous work which this project definitely is. He will need to take breaks or just changes of activity. He might suddenly remember that it is time to water the garden, so he will switch to this activity. Then there would be the time to walk a dog… However, if you are patient, the Water person might be a big boon for you.

Now, before we continue, I'd like you to do a couple of exercises. Later I'll provide the answers but they won't be on this page. Please be patient; don't turn the page.

Imagine this situation: You and your partner/friend came to a party where you know just a few people. What would be your partner's/friend's behavior if he/she is:

Choleric _____
_____
_____

Sanguine _____
_____
_____

Phlegmatic _____
_____
_____

Melancholic_____
_____
_____

Another situation: You've made a mistake in your work, and your boss is giving you a hard time. How would he/she do that, and what would be the best reaction for you if your boss is:

Choleric _____
_____
_____

Sanguine _____
_____
_____

Phlegmatic _____
_____
_____

Melancholic_____
_____
_____

Before discussing the possible answers let's look at the other example (Figure 7), the chart of Audrey Hepburn (just to consolidate the knowledge).

In Fire signs she had Venus and Uranus in Aries, Neptune in Leo and Black Moon (Lilith) in Sagittarius. 1.5+1+1+0.5 = 4.

Air: Mercury in Gemini, Proserpina and White Moon in Libra :1.5+1+0.5 = 3.

Earth: Sun, Jupiter, Chiron and North Moon Node in Taurus, Saturn in Capricorn:

2+1+1+0.5+1 = 5.5.

Water: Moon in Pisces, Mars and Pluto in Cancer, South Moon Node in Scorpio:

2+1+1+0.5 = 4.5.

We can see from the calculation that Audrey Hepburn's strongest element is Earth and the weakest one is Air. However, there is no dominating element in her chart. In order to be the most prominent an element has to have 1.5 times more points than any of the others. Audrey

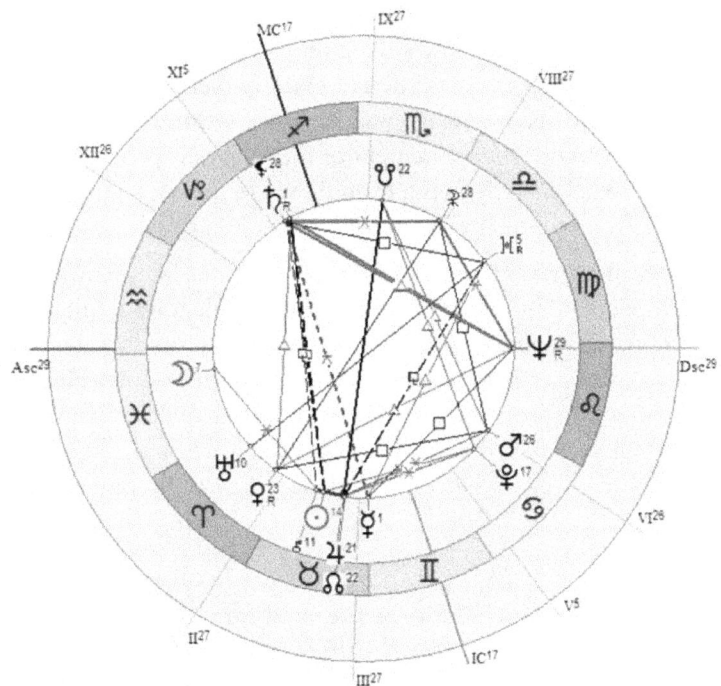

Figure 7: Audrey Hepburn May 4, 1929, 3:00 am GMT -1, Ixelles, Belgium

☉ 13 ♉ 06'	♄ 0 ♑ 02	⚷ 27° ♐ 58'
☽ 6 ♓ 27	♅ 9 ♈ 20	⚴ 27 ♎ 52
☿ 0 ♊ 19	♆ 28 ♌ 35	⊱ 4 ♎ 35 ℞
♀ 22 ♈ 47	♇ 16 ♋ 26	⚸ 10° ♉ 02'
♂ 25 ♋ 09	☊ 21 ♉ 19	Asc 28 ♒ 36
♃ 20 ♉ 45	☋ 21 ♏ 19	Mc 16 ♐ 58

had balanced elements in her chart. If you have balanced elements, we might congratulate you because you have a bit of everything and nothing is completely missing.

Natural Elements and Human Temperaments

OK, now back to our "homework". *The situation with the party.* Both a choleric and a sanguine will be very active in socializing. They will go and talk to strangers. The difference is: a choleric will remember that you are there and try to engage you in conversations; a sanguine might get carried away with the excitement of meeting new people. An Air person will be like a butterfly flying from flower to flower, trying to make an impression. You will be forgotten for a while.

Both phlegmatics and melancholics will not be much into socializing with people they don't know, although a phlegmatic will care much less about other people's opinions. A melancholic might not be happy if you leave him/her behind with a lot of strange people. He will start speaking only if he is introduced to others and they have a mutual interest. An Earth person could be left alone for a while if there is enough tasty food and drinks. Generally both temperaments prefer a circle of close friends.

The work situation example.

If your boss is a choleric, be prepared for a thunderstorm. In case of lack of manners, he can even scream at you or at least won't be able to talk calmly. You just need your patience because Fire people get angry fast but also cool down quickly. The thunder won't last too long. It is better to be silent in the beginning; then, when the steam has been let out, you may talk. If you are a female, in an extreme situation you may even cry a little bit. Fire people can't stand tears; your boss might get embarrassed and "the thunderstorm" will be over sooner.

If your boss is an Air person, there won't be any raised voices. He might still be nice to you but don't get your hopes high: he might call you just to say that you are fired. Sanguines don't like conflicts and will wait as long as possible without talking about trouble. The best reply would be an apology and a sincere promise to correct things. Keep in mind that a sanguine boss might not check for a while if you follow your promises, which gives you some time.

If your boss is a phlegmatic, things are exactly the opposite. Don't give false promises to an Earth person: that makes the situation worse. Your boss will present your mistakes in a calm but firm way and will expect a realistic response. If the source of the problem was beyond your control, your supervisor will understand. If it is completely your mistake, you still can get away with it if you produce a reasonable plan for correcting errors. But remember: he\she will check the result. It is pointless to cry in front of an Earth person (or a sanguine): it won't make any difference.

Frankly speaking, melancholics become supervisors not that often, because they are too sensitive to deal with a lot of people. However, if your boss is a Water person, he might also give you a few chances to correct your mistakes before speaking to you. It isn't easy to give people a hard time. A Water boss might be as stressed out as you are. You should apologize as many times as possible in this case. A Water person might even take into consideration your personal reasons (like relationships, family troubles etc.).

There is no good or bad temperament (or element): everyone is perfect for something. If you want to cry on somebody's shoulder, it is better to choose a Water person. A phlegmatic friend isn't bad either. However, if you try to do this with an Air person, he will tell you: "Come on! Cheer up! Life goes on!" Is this what you want? A Fire person will listen to you but won't offer his\her shoulder. He won't have pity for you but will present you with suggestions as to how to solve the problem. Do you really want to solve the problem? Or just want emotional support?

Do we need to change?

The qualities or characteristics which are present in our horoscope show something important that we were born with. Our chart determines in many ways that we are who we are. However, there are always choices. If you don't like something in your character, you are able to change it. If one of the natural elements is missing from your astrological chart, you still have a possibility to develop it.

There is a way to find out if we need to develop some elements more than others in order to be successful in this lifetime. This method also involves calculations but in this case they are related to the planets in astrological houses. For non-astrologers this part will definitely be more challenging. I'll lead you step-by-step to the result. If you mastered the first calculation, the second one won't be too difficult.

In this particular case we will use exactly the same points for the planets. Instead of signs we will be using houses. The first astrological house starts with Ascendant (ASC), the fourth with Nadir (IC), the seventh with Descendant (DSC) and the tenth with Midheaven (MC). Houses also correspond with elements:

Fire – first, fifth and ninth

Air – third, seventh and eleventh

Earth – second, sixth and tenth

Water – fourth, eighth and twelfth

Let's look at the chart of Vincent van Gogh again (Figure 2) and count planets in the houses.

For the Fire element we can find only Neptune in the ninth house which gives 1.0 point for Fire.

Air: Proserpina (1) in the third house, Pluto (1), Uranus (1), Saturn (1) and Lilith (0.5) in the eleventh house which gives: 1+1+1+1+0.5 = 4.5.

Earth: Moon (2), Jupiter (1), Chiron (1), South Moon Node (0.5) and White Moon (0.5) in the sixth house, Sun (2), Mercury (1.5), Venus (1.5) and Mars (1.5) in the tenth. There are a lot of planets in the Earth houses.

2+1+1+0.5+0.5+2+1.5+1.5+1.5 = 11.5 (for Earth).

Water: North Moon Node is the twelfth house, which is only 0.5.

Now let's see what this calculation can show us. If we compare the signs' elements and the same in the houses, we will get the following:

	Signs	**Houses**
Fire	8.5	1.0
Air	0.5	4.5
Earth	4.5	11.5
Water	4.0	0.5

The elements from the signs side show traits of our character which we were born with. The elements from the houses side represent personal qualities which we will need to accomplish the tasks in our current life.

What kind of conclusion about the above example can we make? Van Gogh had a lot of Fire (the dominant element) which means drive, a hot temper and impatience. However, he didn't need it in his life. Too much Fire for him wasn't good.

He had almost no Air meaning no communication skills, and this really stayed in the way of his career success and his chances of happy relationships. As we can see, he needed Air, although not that much.

Vincent van Gogh had some Earth element but he had to develop much more of it. Earth is the most important element in the houses' system. He had to develop such qualities as patience, persistence, stability and practicality of mind. Van Gogh didn't fulfill this mission, which is why he wasn't as successful in his lifetime as he could have been.

Water was pretty strong according to the signs, but he didn't need it at all. It means no illusions, oversensitivity, self-pity and melancholy. Had he developed the Earth element, it would've never allowed him to be so depressed.

If you decide to calculate elements in the houses' system, you should be sure about the person's birth time (yourself included). Whereas it is unlikely that planets move to a different sign (except the Moon), the houses cusps move pretty fast. If the birth time isn't known, it is pointless to do this calculation.

And that's exactly why I won't do the houses' elements calculation for the example of Audrey Hepburn. The Astro-Databank source gives her time of birth as 3 AM, which I doubt is correct. My doubts are based on discrepancies between her appearance and the first house. As we know, Audrey was exceptionally slim. It wouldn't be possible with the Moon in Pisces on the Ascendant as is shown in her chart (Figure 7). The Moon on ASC usually makes a person plump. There was no roundness in Audrey's figure even in later years. So counting elements in the houses won't give a trustworthy picture. (After I'd finished this book, my friend-astrologer rectified Audrey's birth time for 2:25AM).

If you find out that your elements in both systems are pretty close, consider yourself a lucky one. Developing the missing element is a very difficult task. I know this from personal experience. The strongest element in my birth chart is Water (it is much stronger than any others). I have almost no Fire or Air. Fortunately, I didn't need more Fire but I needed a lot of Air (instead of Water).

I was born a very sensitive, shy girl (Water), who had no idea how to communicate with others properly (shortage of Air). For a big part of my life I was always an outsider. Before I learnt how to develop the Air element in everyday life, I had a lot of painful experience. After the age of twenty-one, I became much better in communicating. Without Air I definitely would not be able to do counseling or teaching.

If one doesn't have enough Earth in their chart but it is required in order to be successful in life, one has to consciously pay attention to being patient and practical. Otherwise, there might be problems, especially in the money area.

Developing the missing Fire element isn't easy either. If one was born with a passive approach in life, then one might find it extremely difficult to change it. Making your own decisions, not waiting for others to make your life better, not being afraid to take a step forward without support and looking back – all of these just sound simple but really could be a huge challenge for people with not enough Fire in their characters.

There is just one more small thing I want to add in this chapter. In some charts planets may be located on the cusp of the house. How to count their points then? For example, Jupiter is in the fifth degree of Cancer and the cusp of the sixth house is in the same degree. In this case 0.5 points go to the Fire element (the fifth house) and another 0.5 to the Earth element (the sixth house). When a planet is on the cusp its points should be evenly divided between neighboring houses.

3

Planets from the Psychological Point of View

After learning about elements and sign's types it makes sense to look closer at the planets. First of all, there are luminaries: the Sun and the Moon, the day luminary and the night one. We might say that the Sun is our spirit and the Moon is our soul. The Sun's position in the sign determines how we call ourselves according to the Zodiac: a Leo, Pisces, Aquarius, Gemini etc. However, there are also eleven other planets and their locations in various signs to be considered.

The Moon is responsible for emotions (which play a huge role in human lives) and subconscious. Exactly through the Moon we can develop deep psychological complexes, and for finding inner balance we'll have to start with her: clearing our subconscious.

The Sun and the Moon as well as Mercury, Venus and Mars are called personal planets. They are generally fast moving and determine the main traits of personality.

Mercury's location in signs shows how we speak and communicate, and the way we think and learn.

Venus (or Aphrodite) is a goddess of love, so it would be logical to assume that she rules the ways of how we can give and receive love. Those ways can be very different for everyone which you can see from the next chapter. Venus is also responsible for our appreciation of beauty and our artistic taste as well as an ability of attracting money and worldly goods.

Mars also has its role in love affairs ruling passion and desires. He is responsible for our way of action (how we fight our life battles) and the strength or weakness of will power.

The next two planets, Jupiter and Saturn, are called social planets. When luminaries and personal planets manifest their energies in the way we reveal ourselves, social planets bring energies for interaction with the world around us.

Jupiter is responsible for our philosophical, ideological and religious beliefs as well as social ambitions and desire to teach or just share one's knowledge in general. Chinese calendar is based on Jupiter cycle: Jupiter spends one year in every sign. People born in the same year, more likely, will share the same social values.

Saturn has very different energy than Jupiter: he is about discipline, self-respect, priorities in life, responsibilities etc. Strong Saturn makes a person extremely goal oriented.

Other planets are transpersonal or co-called planets of generation: Uranus, Neptune, Pluto, Chiron and Proserpina. They are located far from the Sun and, from the Earth vintage point, are very slow. Uranus spends seven years in one sign; people born in those seven years will have the similar qualities of Uranus. Neptune's cycle is 164.79 years, Pluto's 247.7 years. That's why they called planets of generation. All these planets have great importance for life events; however, here we will talk mostly of the qualities they bring into personality (those can be seen only if these planets are strong in the chart).

Uranus gives a person a spark of adventurism, readiness for changes, inventiveness and sometimes some kind of uniqueness and unusual abilities.

Neptune is related to great intuition, unconditional love, musical and psychic abilities but also (if he is unfavorable) to tendency of deception and self-deception.

Pluto is a planet of collective energy, and if he is strong in the chart, he can give some kind of magnetic power as well as excellent survival skills.

I'll describe Chiron and Proserpina in more details because Chiron has a different definition in my astrological school (Avestan School of Astrology, Russia) in comparison to North American astrology and Proserpina is a yet undiscovered planet. There are a lot of sources where you can read about other planets but not these two.

Chiron is an asteroid (or, in fact, the nuclear of a comet) with a cycle close to 51 years. In my astrological school he is considered a planet of balance and harmony. On a personal level he gives diplomacy, an ability to see another person's point of view, fairness and balance. In the worst-case scenario, he can bring hypocrisy, insincerity and an ability of lying plausibly.

Proserpina is an as yet undiscovered planet located beyond Pluto. She is very slow: her cycle is about 665 years. Proserpina passes one degree in 2 years. Ephemeris of Proserpina can be found in Appendix 1.

Proserpina was first introduced by a Russian astrologer, Pavel Globa, who apparently took the concept from ancient East-Indian astrology. For some reason Indian astrologers knew about Proserpina and other father planets long ago, even without modern technology.

Proserpina is responsible for the transformation and irreversible changes in our lives. She is the main planet of medicine, chemistry and alchemy. She should be strong in the charts of the people who work in those fields. Proserpina also gives an ability to see the whole picture while having in hand only random details of it. That's why she is prominent in horoscopes of restorers.

Basically, from a psychological point of view, Proserpina is visible in one's personality only if she was rising in the moment of birth. She can give excellent survival skills and ability for deep inner changes as well as attention to details, patience and willingness to restore order where there is chaos.

4

Venus: What is Love for us?

I am bringing up Venus ahead of other important planets not by chance. Venus represents feelings and love in astrology. And happiness on Earth is not complete without love. Generally, Love is the core of Life. What is Love for you? A pretty tricky question, isn't it? I can't give one answer for this question. Of course, there is unconditional Love, divine Love, but it is so difficult to find it on our earthy level.

Everyone sees love in her/his own way. The way we perceive love, the way we can give and receive it is determined by Venus' position in Zodiac signs. Remember that Venus might be in a different sign than the Sun. It is not the Sun sign but the Venus sign that shows what we expect from love. In fact, Venus is responsible for more life spheres: she plays an important role in our money situation as well as determines our artistic taste. However, here we will be talking mostly about feelings. Let's look more closely at Venus in signs.

Venus in Aries

This is a sign of conquerors or Amazons. Venus here is fast-thinking and enthusiastic. She falls in love quickly, often under the influence of somebody's charming appearance. She is hot-tempered, wants everything right now: a few words of pleasantries and... action! This lack of sophistication definitely won't charm some gentle souls. Venus in Aries doesn't know what compromise is about. Here Venus is in Mars' home, and he dictates: Go and take whatever you want!

She is very sincere in her feelings; that's why it is easy to hurt her. She won't play games and expect the same from the partner. Venus in Aries is passionate and loves a demonstration of affection. Men with this Venus might not treat a lady as a princess; they always see her as an equal. They might not make you change a tire on the car, but they would expect you to enjoy their sports games. The encouraging thing is: they are trainable.

Venus in Taurus

Taurus is Venus' realm; that's why here we have a charming, sensual and artistic Venus (the best Venus qualities). Her feelings are stable and never impulsive. She will create comfort for her loved ones. She tries to avoid boiling passion, ups and downs in emotions. If you are a drama queen, Venus in Taurus won't appreciate this. She seeks harmony and peace in love.

Females with Venus in Taurus are real women. Their men shouldn't forget about this and should shower them with flowers, gifts, dinner invitations etc. This Venus is able to create a beautiful and warm home. However, she can also be very possessive and jealous. She wouldn't share her knight's attention. Above all she needs stability and security.

Venus in Gemini

We might call Venus here a flirtatious Venus. She can be pretty emotional but also has light-hearted feelings. Common sense is always present in her relationships. Venus in Gemini likes intellectual stimulation as much as romance. Love & Friendship – that's how she sees perfect relationships.

She always needs diversity; that's why she might not stay long with the same partner. It is interesting to be with Venus in Gemini, but, in order for her to stay with you, you need to be clever, fascinating, and – at least sometimes – funny, so she won't be bored. This Venus doesn't like routine and sometimes has problems with commitment. Her feelings are always fresh: every love is like the first one.

Venus in Cancer

Venus in Cancer is an extra-sensitive and romantic Venus. There is usually no "love at first sight" for her. You will need time to capture her heart. Since she is in love, she is loyal and much attached to her partner (and her family). This is a compassionate and understanding Venus who can't stand a cold emotional atmosphere at home. She needs the exchange of emotions and warmth in relationships. Venus in Cancer is pretty romantic and likes courting, flowers, strolling on the beach or under the moon, etc. She is very intuitive and charming.

Usually she plays a passive role in love: waiting instead of pursuing. She might have difficulties in revealing her feelings (just because she is afraid). Sometimes Venus in Cancer starts playing one of two roles: a mother or a little girl. This might fulfill her subconscious needs: take care and protect her partner or be protected and spoiled by him/her. Both males and females with Venus in Cancer really need family. However, if a man's Sun is also in Cancer, he might be looking for a woman just exactly like his mother.

Venus in Leo

This is a drama queen. Sorry, people with Venus in Leo, but all of you have it, if only just a little bit. Venus in Leo is capable of very generous love but with a dramatic effect. Here we might have love at first sight (but who know about the second sight or the tenth...). She is an active, impressive, generous and sexual Venus, although she can be demanding (for attention and praise for herself). She is a high-maintenance girl.

Men with Venus in Leo are romantic and charming; very good when it comes to courting. However, don't expect the same from them after the wedding: you might discover that they are cooler with close people and warmer with others (no surprise: they've conquered you, haven't they?) Some people with Venus in Leo are looking for their Galatea: they will do their best to make you successful, fashionable, educated, etc., and then... well, it depends... Galatea has to be endlessly grateful and praise "the master" daily.

A partner's appearance and his/her manners are important for Venus in Leo. It isn't easy to win her love, but Venus in Leo can easily attract love because she is so lovely. However, not everyone can fit into Leo's ardent passion.

Venus in Virgo

A responsible and reasonable Venus, she is in Mercury's home here, so it is no surprise that she borrows some qualities from the host. Venus in Virgo needs intellectual stimulation first. As for passion...well, passion should be measured to prove that it is real. This Venus sometimes seems to be too pragmatic in relationships. She can be calculative and very picky. However, when these people choose a partner, they become devoted, loyal, patient and accommodating. Females usually are very good wives and mothers.

People with Venus in Virgo are excellent in flirting and courting. For the minority of them (mainly men), love is like sport (the more the merrier). They can be critical and pay too much attention to small imperfections. Venus in Virgo sometimes goes to extremes about cleanliness and order in their home, which can be annoying, especially for those with Venus in Fire or Air signs.

Venus in Libra

This is a harmonious, charming, and sophisticated Venus. She usually has high aesthetic standards and creates beauty and comfort around her. Looks and manners are important to her. She usually chooses the same type of partners. Venus in Libra has an inclination to "a golden middle", often liking the same type as others do.

She can't stand pushy people, control freaks and those with bad manners. She doesn't like arguments and fights; she prefers to compromise. This Venus is accommodating, romantic and easy-going. These people are peacemakers in the family and in society.

Venus in Scorpio

Venus in Scorpio is a very passionate and attractive Venus. We can even call her "a femme fatale". There are no limits in love: everything or nothing. Sometimes she sees a partner as an enemy who has to be conquered. This is not an easy-going Venus: she can be too intense, secretive, and pushy. She is magnetic and intriguing. Her look promises a lot and she will give it … if you deserve.

Venus in Scorpio demands ever-lasting passion and commitment. She can be very possessive, jealous and revengeful. This Venus is capable of very deep feelings and can even make sacrifices for love. If hurt, she can carry resentment in her heart for a long time. In this case trust can be an issue for her. If you are in a relationship with Venus in Scorpio, you would not ever be bored.

Venus in Sagittarius

An idealistic, open-minded, and enthusiastic Venus, she thinks that love is all about excitement and adventure, and gets confused when it isn't always like that. She needs mutual ground in relationships: the same philosophical ideas or the same interests. She has an outgoing and even flirtatious nature. This doesn't mean though that she won't go into commitment. However, she will always stay a free spirit.

Venus in Sagittarius sometimes is too bossy and ambitious. You would be better off having the same views as her. She is usually open about her feelings. Even if she loves romantic adventures, she will normally follow the rules of society.

Venus in Capricorn

This is a careful, cautious, and loyal Venus. This Venus is reliable and honest. If she decides that her partner proves worthy, she is ready for a life-long commitment. She will take care of her partner but don't expect her to talk about love (this might happen once in ten years). One of my clients told his wife: "Don't ask me all the time if I love you. I told you once that I do. If it changes, I'll inform you". And they can be pretty honest.

It is difficult for Venus in Capricorn to talk about her feelings. She prefers showing love through her deeds. She is very responsible about her partner and family. Life with her is stable and comfortable but far from romantic. She is also pretty conservative. Often Venus in Capricorn seems cold and distant but, if you look closer, you might find serious sexuality behind the facade. And with age and practice she only gets better.

Venus in Aquarius

This is an independent and detached Venus. She usually has a lot of friends and is a magnetic center of her circle. Generally, friendship for her goes before love. Venus in Aquarius is capable of love at first sight, but this kind of affection might not last long. She doesn't care about one's appearance but only about a unique spark in personality. To attract her you have to be interesting in some way.

People with this Venus are not conservative: they like to try new things in love and life. Freedom is mandatory for them, but they let their partners have it too. They can't stand any pressure or emotional drama. Venus in Aquarius hates boredom and routine; she needs her life to be sparkly and exciting (if you are with her, you will share this lifestyle too). That's why commitment is difficult for her sometimes. It might not be easy finding a partner she prefers. She looks for somebody unique and reliable (because Aquarius is ruled by two very different planets: Uranus (unique) and Saturn (reliable)); two qualities which rarely come together...

Venus in Pisces

This compassionate Venus is capable of unconditional love. Her love is deep, giving and forgiving. Often Venus in Pisces looks for an ideal partner who doesn't exist. Later she might settle for somebody more down-to-earth, but the dream can keep nagging her for the rest of her life. With her idealism she may see the partner as somebody he/she is not.

For this Venus spiritual love comes before the sexual aspect of it. An emotional contact is very important to her. She is very attached to her partner and even might identify herself with her/him. Venus in Pisces is romantic, creative, telepathically tuned to a loved one and generally loyal (well, unless Prince Charming or a beautiful Mermaid come their way). In the worst case scenario, she can be suspicious and moody.

****

With regard to relationships compatibility, Venus in signs should always be brought into consideration. We should not say that people are incompatible if they see love in different ways, but this can definitely create issues in relationships. For example, one partner has Venus in Aries and the other - Venus in Cancer. Reading the above descriptions, you could see a problem right away. A person with Venus in Cancer can't stand the pushiness of Venus in Aries. She/he needs a long "foreplay", but the partner thinks it is not necessary.

I don't think I've ever seen the above combination in a lasting relationship, but I have seen Venus in Pisces and Aries together. I wouldn't say that there were no problems, but somehow, they managed to solve them. If people are open-minded and ready to compromise, they can overcome their differences.

As for other personal planets…I am not going to write about their positions in signs because readers will be able to find a lot of information on the Internet and in books. However, I have to mention the importance of the Moon. The Sun is our spirit, but the Moon is our soul. The Moon sign is also very important, especially for children (before 7 – 8 years of age) and the elderly. The Moon represents our emotions and our subconscious and can add a lot to a personality picture. Little kids often behave according to their Moon sign. In Chapters Five and Six we will talk about the Moon phases and signs.

Mercury is responsible for the ways of communicating, learning and thinking. After learning more about Mercury in signs you might lower your expectations about yourself and your partners\children. We can't expect people with Mercury in Taurus to learn new things quickly, nor can we expect them to be sociable at a young age, but they will remember everything they've learnt. Mercury in Gemini is quick to digest information; Mercury in Cancer or Pisces can't think clearly under emotional stress; Mercury in Scorpio is a bit sarcastic – and nothing can be done about this (unless you really want to).

Mars will show our way of action: fast in Aries, thoughtful but determined in Capricorn, uncertain in Libra, passionate in Scorpio, procrastination-prone in Taurus and so on.

5

Moon Phases and Our Wheel of Reincarnations

The Moon's influence can be pretty significant for one's personality. This planet rules an astral world, which means our emotions, dreams, subconscious, psychic visions etc. The Moon brings energies which we often can't grasp or explain. All mystical stuff, including ghosts and spirits, is related to the Moon. Lunar signs are important, as are lunar phases. Let's talk about phases first.

Moon phases are determined by her position in relation to the Sun. There are four phases: each lasts about seven days. The complete Moon cycle is 29 and one-half days. There are two main parts in the Moon cycle: waxing Moon and waning Moon. New Moon is the beginning of the Moon cycle.

The lunar cycle can also be divided into eight parts which include Crescent Moon, Gibbous Moon, Balsamic Moon etc. Here we'll use only four quadrants plus Full and New Moon. The Moon position in the four quadrants (or phases) is related to our wheel of incarnation (according to the Avestan Astrological School). The closer the waxing Moon is to the

Sun, the younger is the soul on an emotional level. These souls are less experienced and more innocent; they are excited, like kids, about new emotional adventure. People of the waning Moon, especially those of the last quarter, are more experienced in all manifestations of the astral world. They are more like adults or even the elderly because they had some bitter experience in their past lives. Experience and understanding don't necessarily make us happier; it is often exactly the opposite.

Every phase has its mythological image. According to the concepts of ancient people, who liked symbols a lot, the world is standing on four elephants that represent four Moon phases ruling our subconscious. All elephants have their own colours: red, yellow, blue and green (colours are not given by chance). In ancient Greece lunar phases were ruled by four Goddesses.

First Moon Phase

You were born in the first Moon quarter if it happened within seven days from the new Moon (from the Sun-Moon conjunction to the first Sun-Moon square). The first lunar phase has the earth element, and its Goddess is the virgin Goddess-hunter, Artemis. The colour is blue, the colour of virginity.

Those born in the first phase have some innocence or immaturity about their emotional reactions. Everything is new to them. Often, they are unaware of what their impressions really mean to them on an emotional level, and it can take a lot of time for them to figure out what is happening on a subconscious level. There is no surprise because they just started learning. These people are open to any outer influence but at the same time they have inner resistance. Usually, their psyche is stable (earth element) and balanced.

People of the first lunar phase can be very active and overly enthusiastic. The Moon is still very close to the Sun, and solar rays can blind a person. When these people make mistakes, they sometimes go unpunished because of their inexperienced soul: they are still considered kids in the Universe.

Usually, people born in the first Moon phase don't take anything too close to their heart (unless the Moon is in the Water signs); here their reactions are completely opposite to the people of the fourth lunar phase. The first quarter people have a lot of hidden potential which they still have to discover.

It is a different story if a person was born on the border of the first and second Moon quarters. Here the Moon gets first stress from the Sun: a square aspect – 90 degrees. People who have this aspect in their charts can be painfully sensitive and they usually have enough stress in their lives to learn from it. For those people, this incarnation is the stage of choices, transformation, the beginning of understanding their subconscious motives and searching for emotional balance.

Second Moon Phase

This phase is connected to the Water element. The colour is green. Selene, the goddess of the Moon, is the symbol of this phase. According to some sources, the patroness of the Moon in the second quarter can also be Thetis, the goddess of water.

In the second phase the Moon starts showing all her beauty. If we recall that the Moon represents femininity, we might guess that this phase is especially favourable for women. For example, in old Japan the search for new geisha was focused on girls of the first and second lunar phases. They were deemed most preferable because they could show the best feminine qualities and were emotionally stable. I believe that in India there were the same preferences in searching for wives.

The Moon in the second phase has more experience but still not enough for being independent. People of this phase are pretty sensitive, astute and intuitive, but usually don't show their emotions; their emotions don't go ahead of their minds. If people of the first lunar quarter need comfort, the second phase's individuals must have an emotional interaction. They can't exist in a cold emotional atmosphere. It isn't easy for these people to relax.

People of the waxing Moon are still learning to open their real emotional nature. After the full Moon things will change drastically.

Via Lunaris – the Full Moon

There are four special days between the second and third quarters when our night luminary can be seen in her entire beauty. These days of the full Moon were also called Via Lunaris (the Moon road). In this time the Moon and the Sun are in opposition or very close to this aspect.

This is the time when the Moon becomes independent from the Sun. People born on Via Lunaris have the greatest emotional freedom; however, it is necessary to know how to use it. This special Moon position might make individuals unbalanced because their spirit (the Sun) and soul (the Moon) are in some kind of conflict (the opposition). These people can be moody; their emotional reactions changing all the time. They are also easy to influence because their souls are open to everything – both good and bad. They can be unpredictable and sometimes very superstitious.

The main task for full-Moon people is learning how to be truly free and independent. If they learn to be rational and irrational at the same time, to develop both their conscious and subconscious parts simultaneously, they can be balanced and use the Moon energy in the best possible way. People of Via Lunaris are very sensitive and intuitive; they usually have interesting dreams that are almost prophetic in nature. There are a lot of psychics and people who do channelling among them.

People born in the full Moon and new Moon are usually sensitive to lunar phases, especially to the full Moon. When the Moon is in the sky in her entire glory, people might become anxious and nervous without reason, and their sleep is disturbed. If you have those symptoms and they happened in the full Moon, be patient: they will be gone in a couple of days.

Third Moon Phase

This phase was named after the goddess Dione and is related to the Air element. The colour is yellow. Dione is the gods' ambassadress; she brings their will to humans.

Here the Moon is waning, losing her brightness. People of this phase start losing their emotional freedom. Generally, these individuals have more experience on a subconscious level than people of the waxing Moon. They can be imbalanced and lose more on an emotional level than they gain.

In terms of compensation, they need a lot of social contact. People of the third Moon phase can be changeable and unpredictable, as well as very talkative, and sometimes shallow and fussy (in the worst-case scenario). However, if they learn how to focus, they can become great thinkers and inventors. Their thinking process never stops, and they are very sensitive to the thoughts and ideas of others. They can keep their thoughts always clear and unbiased.

Even when they play the social butterfly, we shouldn't forget that those born in the third Moon phase are often pretty touchy and might have a painful reaction to words they think inappropriate.

Fourth Moon Phase

This phase has the Fire element and the colour red, the colour of blood. Its goddess is Gorgona (Gorgon), the goddess of vengeance.

A person born in the fourth quarter has gone through a lot in his\her reincarnations. These people are the most emotionally experienced. They have very mature emotions. They are brave, unafraid of receiving emotional pain, and ready to fight. Sometimes they can be impulsive and rough. Individuals of the fourth phase don't always control their emotional reactions and usually don't know what they are capable of.

The fourth Moon quarter brings emotional "overload" and suppression simultaneously. Those born in this phase can be impatient and tend to overreact. Sometimes even a small irritation can make them explode. Their subconscious reactions frequently overwhelm their rational mind. It is very difficult to influence these people; they can't be controlled, preferring to rely on their own experience exclusively.

Individuals of the fourth lunar phase are very strong but they need to learn what to do with this strength and how to control their emotional reactions.

The New Moon

There are four days of the dark Moon, right before and after the new Moon (the beginning of the new Moon cycle). This time also has its own goddess – Hekate. Hekate is related to magic, witchcraft, hidden treasures, fears and psychological complexes. Ancient astrologers considered these days special, strange, and mystical.

In the new Moon the power of the subconscious is extremely strong. That's why people born in this time might have a lot of things – on a subconscious level – they are not even aware of (hidden fears, for example). The new Moon's people are as sensitive as the people of Via Lunaris, but they are also very reserved and don't show their emotions.

People of the dark Moon can be very spiritual and can make good psychics, but they also have a vulnerable soul, so they should be careful with any esoteric practices.

The four days of the new Moon are very different. The two before the actual new Moon are very difficult. The emotional experiences those people carry can be just overwhelming. After the new Moon, starting a new cycle, things are a bit better. Individuals of the last two days of the dark Moon can be naïve, but that is never the case for people of the first two Hekate's days (still a waning Moon). People born in the new Moon are as sensitive to the Moon's cycles as those born in the days of the full Moon.

6

Moon in Signs – The Mirror World of Our Soul
The Distortion of Reality and Our Fears

The Moon is a passive luminary dependent on the Sun. She is just a mirror which reflects our emotional reactions to life's events. As you know, the same kinds of events bring different sorts of reactions from different people. There is always much more to any event than we can perceive. Being a mirror, the Moon can distort the perceptible reality; how – depends on the Moon sign.

You might agree that our emotional reactions are always subjective. Only because of our emotional reactions is the forming of psychological complexes possible (more on this subject in Chapter Eight). The formation of complexes always begins with the Moon: from emotions generated by stressful situations (even very small events); then, with the help of Saturn, those emotions may (or may not) be transformed into complexes.

Carl Jung described complexes as an unconscious, repressed, yet highly influential symbolic material that is incompatible with consciousness. These psychic substances can act completely independently and sometimes surprise our conscious mind with the outcome.

Not every crisis or upsetting situation will lead to the formation of a complex. In order for this to happen, one has to have a very sensitive and susceptible personality. The status of the Moon and her position in the signs will show if this is the case. Causes of negative complexes also include the inability or unwillingness of a person to accept his\her nature. Those unwanted psychological elements are forced out of consciousness and become an active part of the subconscious.

The Moon's position in the four main elements determines the nature of possible complexes. You will recall, from Chapter Two, that elements (Water, Fire, Earth and Air) form the core of our personality. We will look more closely at the Moon's position in those elements and in signs as well. (I used the work of Olga Lomakina, Russian astrologer and psychologist, in the part regarding the connection between elements and possible emotional complexes).

Moon in Fire Element

The Fire Moon tries to resemble the Sun. She tries to prove that she is bright, independent and unbiased. People with this Moon are harsh and dramatic in their reactions and quite often think that they know what is right for everyone. They can't accept that every person might have her/his own truth. Because of this disposition, they willingly interfere in the lives of others, imposing their own solutions to everyone's problems.

The most common complex for people with the Moon in Fire signs is an inferiority complex, which is the source of their other complexes. If a person is extra ambitious and/or has a mania of self-greatness, then the roots of all these traits could be found in an inferiority complex. This complex often manifests itself through aggression (both inner and outer) and inadequate and dramatic reactions.

Quite often, complexes grow in the ground of impulses and emotions which were forced into the subconscious. With regard to the Fire element, those emotions are related to any kind of personal failure. Matters that we can't accept have nowhere else to go, only hiding deep inside. Failure is not acceptable for people of the Fire Moon.

Moon in Aries

The Moon in this sign, ruled by Mars, usually has a "black/white" perception; nothing in between. Subconsciously these people are always ready to fight. They can be very idealistic as well as impulsive, brave, active, harsh with words and self-assured.

Despite their outer self-confidence, some of them can have an inferiority complex that usually manifests itself through doubts about the rightness of their choices and the perception of their personal value for partners and for society. The Moon in Aries (as well as in other Fire signs) always fights her complexes. To mask their uncertainty these people might aggressively push their opinion onto others, even if they are not sure if it is right.

It is the same with relationships: it is very important for them to be right, just to prove to themselves that they are worthy. Individuals with Aries Moon can't stand their own failures and will suffer from them for a long time, until they forget about it or try to prove to themselves and others that everything was other than it really was.

Moon in Leo

Here the Moon is in the Sun's realm. Her mirror reflects a pure Sun light. People with this Moon have an open heart; they are very sincere. They always give preference to those situations where they can manifest their inner self. These people usually are good actors, subconsciously adding a dramatic effect to their behavior. They want to share their emotional experience with others and it is important for them that others notice their feelings. In short, the inner world of someone with the Moon in Leo should be the center of the Universe.

The psychological complex of Leo's Moon shows in hidden anxiety about the inability to open their deep and beautiful inner world. They need people to see its richness and perfectness. "If they don't, they won't love me", is the fear lurking in their subconscious. They need everybody to love them, and they begin by attracting attention.

Individuals with Leo's Moon are usually bright and charming. In order to grab others' attention they may show off, sometimes embarking on risky adventures. All they need is empathy and recognition. They can tolerate hatred much better than oblivion.

Moon in Sagittarius

Jupiter is the ruler of Sagittarius and gives the Moon the subconscious knowledge of authority, hierarchy and social relations. People with this Moon often have an inner feeling of self-importance; they want to be an example for others; to teach them. These individuals have subconscious knowledge of how to behave in order to attract respect. In the worst-case scenario, they are arrogant, super-ambitious and pompous.

The mirror reflection of this Moon shows a possible inferiority complex developing through painful doubts about the rightness of one's ideas and conceptions. An individual with this Moon might show this complex through the perception that his/her accomplishments are not appreciated nor recognized properly.

Sagittarius is a pretty ambitious sign. However, behind the mirror showing a demand for recognition there are doubts about the sufficiency of one's knowledge and the deserving of one's authority. If there is already a complex, meaning it is dwelling in the subconscious unnoticed, then it tempts and provokes that person. The fear of their own inferiority can create arrogance, pride and delusions of grandeur.

If the complex hasn't been formed yet, meaning the person doesn't have a strong experience in this area (recognition of his authority, etc.), then the anxiety of his worthiness still can be accessed by the conscious mind. In this case a person can simply add to their knowledge, information and experience, so that later he can teach others. People with the Moon in Sagittarius should be aware of situations where their knowledge is questioned (like losing position in a dispute because the opponent was stronger). They might feel shocked about this experience and, if they don't take care of their feelings right away, those emotions might go deep into their subconscious, forming a complex.

In the worst-case scenario, this complex gives amazing arrogance accompanied by the humiliation of being dependent.

Moon in Air Element

The main distortion of the Air Moon's mirror is related to connections between parts and the whole structure of the surrounding world. A person with the Air Moon will be concerned with sensibility, proportions and the rationality of the outside world. When this person meets something (another person, an event, a book, anything), his / her first reaction will be to establish the connection of this experience to the world, unity, the whole, the Universe.

In order to understand connections, people of the Air Moon need a lot of information and time for its digesting. If they don't understand the meaning of processes, they become anxious. Any emotional traumas might be long to heal for the Air Moon and might lead to difficult, hidden complexes. In this case, instead of being rational, people become very emotional.

The main complex of this Moon is related to movement and time, to obstacles and the ending of some processes. Overall, it can be the fear of death – not exactly one's own, but the death of something around them. These people are afraid of stopping, of the moment when everything comes to an end, the end of life. This complex might show itself through some irritation or neurasthenic reactions. Generally, people of the Air Moon are not prone to hysterics but they have a lot going on inside.

The main dissonance of Air is its duality: they need to comprehend separation and unity at the same time.

Moon in Gemini

Because the Moon here is in Mercury's realm, rational and emotional reactions are interlaced. Gemini Moon is mobile, changeable, flexible and adaptable, as well as sensitive. People with this Moon are excellent transmitters of any kind of information. They are usually social creatures. Subconsciously they are always tuned to change, looking for new experiences and information. People with Gemini Moon hate routine and some of them can be unstable and unreliable.

The main complex of Gemini Moon grows from the fear of difficulties and obstacles on the path of some sensible and important idea or process. Actually, it grows mainly from the expectation of obstacles in the way of a super-important process. People get nervous and begin creating roundabout routes just in case of possible difficulties (plan B, C, D, etc.). It might even lead to subconscious changes, doubts and hesitations. People may look for additional contacts in terms of security, and, in the worst-case scenario, might give their power to other people or circumstances.

Gemini Moon tries being rational; however, when personal relationships interfere, she might lose her rationality and become extra-sensitive. When people with the Gemini Moon are nervous, the evidence can be seen in their hands: biting nails, picking something off or scratching, etc.

Moon in Libra

People with the Moon in Libra are pretty sociable with an inner sense of balance and justice, and excellent artistic taste. They are peaceful souls (unless there is a lot of Fire in their horoscope) who try to avoid confrontations. Compromise is their way of dealing with other people. They are very good diplomats.

Although they are generally not judgmental, these people can often be subconsciously choosy about their social circle, preferring to belong to a narrow circle of some kind of "elite". Individuals with the Moon in Libra can't stand bad manners. They can be judgmental about events and opinions and can't help considering how occurrences correspond with their inner feeling of proportion and justice. Disproportion and ugliness can literally hurt them.

The complex of this Moon is also related to a fear of the end of processes, of death. The Libra Moon isn't a warrior's Moon, but people who have it try using qualities available to them to make sure that the life they envisioned is in place. Those qualities are diplomacy, high personal responsibility and tact. Sometimes fear makes them compromise too much and, if they allow the imperfections of the world to bother them a lot, people with this Moon might become pessimistic and even depressed.

Moon in Aquarius

This Moon gives implacability to conservative tendencies, limitations on freedom and generally any kind of regulation. The soul of such a person is independent and freedom loving. They are nice and friendly towards everyone, but their relations always have an impersonal character. Aquarius Moon has a strange combination of altruism and egoism. These people are usually loyal in friendship but keep themselves a bit distant. They are very inventive and crave anything new.

Individuals with the Aquarius Moon have even stronger fear than other Air Moons: fear of the future. They are afraid that changes won't come. They care about humankind as a whole and worry that changes for the better for everyone won't happen as fast as they should.

Among individuals with the Moon in Aquarius we can find a lot of intelligent and unbiased people who have impersonal kindness. However, in the worst-case scenario, they are very changeable to the point of being unreliable, eccentric, undependable and capricious.

Moon in Water element

The Moon's in Water mirror distorts reality in the area of self-preservation, which is considered super-important and super-valuable. When this person looks at reality, he sees first something that might threaten his life support.

Another type of complex is that of failure, which sometimes shows itself through the complex of impracticality. In the worst-case scenario, a lot of fears and hysterical reactions are possible.

It is no surprise that water signs are very sensitive and take everything close to their heart. The Water Moon is famous for her deep emotions, excellent intuition, instinctive reactions and a great role of the subconscious. People see these individuals as emotionally unstable, which isn't considered fortunate. However, there is still a little bit of good in this: these individuals are also unstable and changeable when it comes to stereotypes and complexes, making the formation of complexes more difficult.

Any negative emotional experience which may start a serious complex turns first into numerous little complexes and brings stormy inner processes for Water Moon people. Those emotional reactions often open new horizons and create new perceptions and, overall, make people more adaptable. Sometimes even negative emotional experiences can be beneficial for the Water Moon. The emotional reaction for her is more important than the object which created this reaction. Because of the liquid nature of Water, one emotional reaction can flow into another, quickly. If people of this Moon don't dwell in the past, they may avoid complexes.

However, if they experienced real, life-threatening situations and were unable to deal with them right away, those memories would be removed from the conscious mind to the deep subconscious and stay there, sometimes creating nightmares, irrational fears, etc.

Moon in Cancer

Cancer is the realm of the Moon in which she can fully manifest herself. This Moon gives sensitivity, excellent intuition and imagination, psychological abilities as well as restraint, moodiness and a suspicious mind. Often a person with the Moon in Cancer can feel another person's energy on a very deep, subconscious level.

Normally, the inner world for these people is more important than the outer one. They feel the influence of cosmic rhythms and Moon phases; their psyche is mobile and changeable. They are touchy and can open up only to the people they trust. If they don't have enough attention and warmth in real life, they create their own fantasy world and seriously protect it from intrusion.

The Moon in Cancer can have a complex of social success and social recognition. The very thought that achieving some goals might not be possible makes individuals with this Moon very anxious and nervous. They think a lot about possible failure and they worry too much. Because of their emotional attitude towards goals and social success, it is difficult for them to distinguish the main and the secondary in the definition of the goal. People with the Moon in Cancer can develop a lot of fantasies as a compensatory mechanism.

Despite huge sensitivity, this Moon is not inclined to forming deep complexes. She won't let negative experiences go deep in her subconscious because her reaction to stress is immediate. Despite the fact that people with the Cancer Moon look very emotional, in reality they have pretty good survival skills.

Sometimes, though, if they let their subconscious take an upper hand, they might become reserved and suspicious. Quite often people with this Moon are not satisfied with superficial social relations and try to move them to a deeper personal level. They are often hurt by the impossibility of this.

Moon in Scorpio

Scorpio is the fall sign for the Moon; its rulers are Pluto and Mars. The Moon in Scorpio subconsciously is tuned to situations of crisis, destruction and transformation. People with this Moon can be very tough on themselves as well as on others. They can be critical and unforgiving.

The Scorpio Moon brings a gift of being good in psychology. Individuals with this Moon can deeply feel the inner world of a person, his strengths, weaknesses and "red buttons". Those individuals make good psychologists or psychiatrists, as well as mediums and psychics.

In the worst-case scenario, they may use their abilities in manipulation to get what they want. The Scorpio Moon can also bring sarcasm and pessimism.

A complex of this Moon is the power complex. These people have to be involved everywhere and, if possible, have control. A psychological part of these people has to be active. The mirror of the Scorpio Moon needs to reflect many people. Such individuals require a lot of emotional interaction – the more intense, the better. If there is no suitable environment for expressing emotions and their own subconscious perception of reality, the Moon in Scorpio can become gloomy and passive with no motivation for action.

People with the Scorpio Moon like power but, when it comes to creating a stable and successful material base (money, property, investments), they might show impracticality and a lack of resourcefulness. Power usually comes with money, and if they don't master the materialistic aspect, they will be disappointed.

Scorpio Moon likes to experience emotional/psychological situations on the borderline: exciting, critical and even extreme. Overcoming them gives her power and high self-esteem. That's why sometimes people with this Moon create critical situations for their "entertainment". That's exactly where Drama Queens – or Kings – come from.

Moon in Pisces

Pisces are ruled by Neptune and Jupiter. Neptune gives depth, intuitive understanding of hidden global processes along with harmony, mysticism and idealism. People with this Moon (even fire and earth signs) have amazing intuition (although earth and fire signs may not trust it) as well as sensitivity. This Moon can be sentimental and easy to influence, or she might try to hide the deepness of the inner world from others.

The Moon in Pisces is never active and can be very attached and ready for self-sacrifice. Their idealism might play a bad joke on these people. No perfect world exists, and in searching for it they can take a wrong approach in looking for a substitute.

The most common complex for the Moon in Pisces is related to self-preservation in society. Concepts about social duties and obligations might become sources of anxiety. There can be two extremes. One group with the Moon in Pisces (especially women) can't find their place in society (quite often with no reason). They focus on their family life instead. In the other case scenario, they might form a complex from social obligations; it is easy for them because Pisces is the sign that always is eager to help. There might be too much self-sacrifice, a lot of guilt (again, with no reason) and trying to help others when they are not asked.

This Moon can also be very creative, which is why we find a lot of artists, singers, musicians, psychics and spiritual people with this Moon in their charts.

Moon in Earth element

The mirror of the Earth Moon has its own distortion of reality. This Moon is very attached to forms: either physical forms or thoughts and concepts or something else. The main feature of such forms is stability – as well as firmness and precision. Being an inert element, Earth tries to preserve forms at any cost. There is no space for change. Stability is super-valuable.

People with this Moon think that their emotional responses should be structured. From the outside, the Earth Moon looks stable, reliable, solid and reasonable; however, those who are close to these people know that this is just a façade. The Earth Moon can be very unstable, bringing sudden mood changes which might go from cold inaccessibility to passionate and stormy emotions.

A mask of coolness is important for these people. However, if someone or something threatens to destroy or simply shake their precious forms, they may show inappropriately strong emotions. Loss of the customary stereotypes can be very emotionally painful for the Earth Moon. That's why the main complex of people with this Moon is based on the fear of change. Earth Moon people try to structure life in general, both its visible and invisible aspects. Their possible complexes might be stable but not overly destructive.

Moon in Taurus

This is one of the best positions for the Moon. Here she is in exaltation, on her throne. People with this Moon are usually emotionally adequate, stable and calm, with a phlegmatic temperament. They are very attached to comfort (good food, cozy home, etc.) and harmony. They can be lost in inharmonious situations.

Their peaceful nature and tendency to slow reactions prevent complexes from being created quickly. There is a certain period of time between an emotional trigger and a responsive reaction, which is why it takes time for complexes to appear. But if it has happened, it is extremely difficult to get rid of them. The Moon in Taurus might bring complexes only if she has major stressful aspects (square and opposition).

Taurus Moon more than any other Earth Moon is inclined to create forms which can be material or mental. After finishing this creation, people with this Moon start worrying about its possible destruction. If there is already a complex, then it may show itself through strengthening the power over created forms, including emotional pressure. Relationships are one of those forms. Taurus, in general, is known as a very possessive sign. People with the Moon in Taurus will do their best to make a relationship extra stable. However, in extreme cases, when the complex is very strong and a person can't deal with it, this person is able to destroy their own creation.

Moon in Virgo

Here the Moon is in the realm of Mercury and Proserpina. Mercury gives her rationality and Proserpina imparts attention to detail. People with this Moon can see the smallest details at first glance and can easily detect discrepancies. Responsibility is installed in their subconscious. They can also be picky, fastidious and petty. They rarely express their emotions.

The imperfection of the world, which these people easily see, is based on the contradiction between rational and irrational. Often their complexes are built around the fear of unknown, mysterious, incomprehensible and non-material things, which helps in explaining the existence of many scientists, researchers and detectives with Virgo Moon. They can delve into the deep unknown and make impressive discoveries. Sometimes the motivation for this lays in the fear of the incomprehensible and invisible which should be studied and explained.

Virgo Moon people often try to balance the themes of God and Nature. They prefer to deal with tangible objects. When experiencing stressful situations related to the invisible and mysterious world, they might become emotionally unstable, very superstitious as well as timid and obedient, which makes them easy to manipulate.

Moon in Capricorn

The host for the Moon in Capricorn is Saturn. Saturn is a very serious guy and immediately suggests austerity, closeness and the possibility of late emotional development. Saturn generally limits any kind of manifestations, resulting in a lot of feelings and emotions just staying buried inside. The Moon in this sign is very reasonable: she always asks a question: can those emotional reactions help me in reaching my determined goals? If not, forget them. Capricorn's Moon hates feeling vulnerable.

The emotional reactions of this Moon are stable, as are its complexes. Capricorn is a cardinal sign, and if a complex somehow managed to develop, it will stay there. This could happen because these people are very attached to stereotypes. Of course, they also have good qualities: determination, reliability and steadfastness. If there is a complex, all of these can be turned into vulnerabilities.

The main fear that "helps" in the formation of a complex is the fear of the future (and time in general). That's why people with Capricorn's Moon love schedules, plans, etc., so much. They always memorize their emotionally negative experiences and try never to get in the same situation again. Dealing with them can be pretty challenging for people who are close to them. Persons with the Moon in Capricorn, as well as with other earthy Moons, could break long-lasting relationships easily and never look back.

On the other side, the Moon in Capricorn is so concerned about the future that she is always ready to do her best to help in its formation. They can become so obsessed with overcoming obstacles and difficulties that they wouldn't recognize that those obstacles are not there yet (and that their preventive measures would be of no help).

7

Mercury – See Who Is Talking?

When people ask me: "Guess what sign I am", I never take the bait. The reason for that is the fact that when you first meet a person your perception of him\ her isn't based on the Sun sign but on the rising sign or the Mercury position. The way in which we talk and communicate is what makes the first impression. Mercury is the closest to the Sun planet (although there is one closer but yet undiscovered – Vulcan) which rules our way of thinking and talking. Because Mercury is so close to the Sun, he can't go far from our star relative to the Earth's vantage point. In your chart Mercury can be only in the Sun's sign or in two neighboring signs.

Parents should know about their kids' Mercury positions because then they can understand should there be any problems with speech or communications and what kind of issue – if any. Parents might see how their children will do in school, especially in the early years when the children lack personal awareness. The below-listed position of Mercury in signs might give you some insights.

Mercury in Aries

Mercury in Aries can be impatient, intolerant and impulsive. People with this position talk first and then think. However, they are also fast learners and enthusiastic in studying things they are interested in. Teachers might complain that such kids have no attention, but that isn't always true: those children grasp ideas quickly and don't like repetition.

Mercury in this sign gives sharpness of mind and strong opinions, which is why these people have problems with compromise and are often found having heated discussions. They are also very enthusiastic about trying new things but seem not to have the patience to continue doing them. They want everything right now and can't wait. Being headstrong, Mercury in Aries often jumps to conclusions without analyzing all the facts.

In the worst-case scenario, individuals with Mercury in Aries can be rude. Kids with this Mercury should be taught to respect other human beings from an early age. If you want them to understand your point of view, don't argue or interrupt them; let them say everything they want to say and then patiently, but firmly, speak about your ideas.

Mercury in Aries is generally good for scientists.

Mercury in Taurus

Mercury in Aries was visiting the Mars' sign; the hostess of Taurus is Venus. Mercury here is completely different: slow, conservative, rational and patient. Teachers would not complain about these kids being inattentive but might say that those students are slow in grasping ideas and need many repetitions. Yes, Mercury in Taurus might be a slow learner, but once he gets the information it will stay in his mind forever.

This Mercury won't jump to conclusions; he will make sure that he gathers all data on the subject before presenting his opinion. While Mercury in Aries makes sure that his opinions are known, Taurus' Mercury isn't so eager in this regard. However, it is Mercury in Taurus whose ideas people take seriously because they are not harsh and are always thought through.

In communications, Taurus' Mercury is pretty conservative. People with this Mercury are those who still have their high school friends around come retirement age.

Mercury in Gemini

This Mercury likes talking and can talk a lot. Gemini is one of the most talkative signs; its only competitor is Sagittarius. Such people's minds are flexible and quick, but a bit impatient. They are fast learners but can lose interest quickly. Teachers might complain about kids with Mercury in Gemini that they are a disturbance in the class because they always try talking to their classmates; however, even those teachers would admit that the kids don't need much time to grasp ideas.

Mercury in Gemini loves new things but, again, tends to lose interest quickly. He doesn't have patience to go deep into the subject, so his approach might seem a bit shallow. These people want to know about everything…but just a bit. Even if the student with Gemini's Mercury doesn't know much about a subject, he/she can talk a lot around and around it, such that the teacher finally gives a good mark even if just out of tiredness.

What is really great about this Mercury is his open-mindedness. These people are not conservative; they are always open to new ideas. At the same time, they are pretty rational and practical. They might be easy to influence, but not for long. The best of this Mercury is the fact that he is a transmitter of ideas.

This position of Mercury is very beneficial for translators, journalists and salespeople.

Mercury in Cancer

Here we have a very sensitive, emotional and intuitive mind. People with this Mercury are very selective in what they want to learn, although they can learn any subject perfectly. However, when they are done with it, their subconscious part might give an order: "Forget. We will never need it". And they will forget.

Mercury in Cancer can be shy in communications. He can open up only in the emotionally warm environment. If there is no understanding they won't talk. Sometimes they understand others without them saying a word. As much as Mercury in Gemini is a transmitter, Mercury in Cancer is a receiver.

People with Mercury in Cancer have a good sense of humor; they are funny copycats. They have an excellent imagination and can be both open to new ideas and conservative (but they will also change old ideas to suit a current moment).

This position of Mercury is good for psychologists, writers and historians.

Mercury in Leo

Here we have a creator of ideas and those ideas are bright. There are so many ideas in these people's minds that they generously share them with others, knowing that they won't be able to realize all these projects themselves. Mercury in Leo as well as in Aries creates people who are wonderful public speakers who share their enthusiasm with their audience.

The individual with Leo's Mercury is idealistic, creative and charismatic, and has sense of purpose; the one whom others will follow. However, Mercury in Leo needs attention and admiration; otherwise, he might become bored and dull. Even if the idea isn't theirs – but one they believe in – these people can easily convince others to follow.

Teachers might describe children with this Mercury as bright and insightful, born leaders who can also easily lose interest and who like to show-off.

Mercury in Virgo

Virgo is Mercury's second realm (the first is Gemini); this is a very strong position for this planet. People with this Mercury have a practical, critical and precise mind, strong logic and common sense, good memory and great attention to detail. They tend to follow the rules; that's why they might become teachers' favorites. However, it could end if they start catching teachers making mistakes (they can be extra pedantic).

Mercury in Virgo is an excellent position for researchers. Everything in their brain is on the proper shelf. Individuals with Virgo's Mercury are excellent in analysis but not so good in synthesis. Sometimes they are lacking creativity. There is a tendency to over-intellectualize life patterns. They are good at talking, especially about practical matters.

People with Mercury in Virgo are quite often perfectionists, leading them to worry a lot. They feel safe only if everything is thought through in advance and well-prepared. A mental overload might impair their digestive system.

In addition to researchers, this Mercury's position is beneficial for accountants, computer programmers and technicians.

Mercury in Libra

Mercury in the sign of balance will weigh both sides of any issue many times in order to make a perfect choice. The fact that perfection is unreachable doesn't trouble him. Don't expect quick decisions from people with Mercury in Libra. These people are pretty sociable and diplomatic; however, they also can be picky about their contacts.

They like to know a little bit of everything. The best of them might have an encyclopedic knowledge; others can be superficial. Their mind wants harmony; they like to be in a "golden middle". Individuals with Libra's Mercury always have a strong opinion about everything but might not voice it in order not to disturb the peace. They are ready for a compromise and sometimes compromise too much because they hate fights. Usually they are polite and tactful.

In the worst-case scenario, they always go with the flow, don't make efforts to achieve results and compromise their values in order to be liked by everyone.

This Mercury position is good for diplomats, lawyers and waiters.

Mercury in Scorpio

Mercury in Scorpio is focused on results. A no-nonsense guy, his mind is bound with intuition and can get to the roots of all things. Usually they don't have a lot of contacts because they are picky and not many people are able to handle them.

Individuals with Scorpio's Mercury often have a dark sense of humor, can be sarcastic and lack diplomacy. They like to argue and can "kill" with their words. The lower-developed persons are judgmental and over-critical, with a negative view of life. They also can be suspicious, hypochondriac and obsessive.

People with this Mercury like mystery; they have a researcher's mind and the human psyche is especially interesting to them. They do a lot of self-analysis. There are many excellent psychotherapists and psychiatrists with Mercury in Scorpio, as well as detectives and esoteric teachers.

Mercury in Sagittarius

Mercury in this sign is open-minded but not revolutionary. He prefers to keep to the beaten track and listen to recognized authorities. People with Sagittarius' Mercury love to learn and are very enthusiastic about new ideas. However, they don't have the patience to explore those ideas in depth and convert them into something practical. They get carried away with brand new projects and drop the old ones.

Individuals with this Mercury are very sociable and probably the most talkative people of all Zodiac signs. They have a good sense of synthesis but not analysis (the opposite to Virgo). Generally very optimistic people, sometimes they are overly optimistic and like to exaggerate their successes.

They sometimes speak first and then think. Such individuals need constant intellectual stimulation but also need to control their restlessness and not change subjects too often. Getting practical results is difficult for them.

People with Mercury in Sagittarius are good with languages; they can be successful travel agents, teachers, priests, missionaries and philosophers.

Mercury in Capricorn

Being in the realm of Saturn, Mercury in Capricorn is organized and focused. He knows where he is going and how he will get there. He is practical, cautious, methodical and often conservative. A person with this Mercury won't talk just for the sake of it: he always has something worthy to say (at least, from his point of view). He has a good memory and often good math ability. In school he is known not for speed but for stable learning.

Quite often people with Capricorn's Mercury are perfectionists who tend to underestimate their own achievements. Their type of communication sometimes seems dry and reserved. They also can be narrow-focused and inclined to a negative point of view. These people can be pessimistic, which they see as being realistic.

This position of Mercury is favorable for scientists, politicians and philosophers.

Mercury in Aquarius

Mercury in this sign can give a bright intellect and unorthodox, sometimes eccentric, mind. He has diverse interests. People with Aquarius' Mercury are usually very open-minded, friendly and helpful. They might have pretty unusual hobbies. They hate discipline but demand it from others.

Grasping abstract ideas is their strong point. Generally, they prefer theory to practice.

If kids with this Mercury are too independent, it might cause problems at school. They might choose to be an outcast or demonstrate shocking behavior instead of being like everybody else. They can be open and honest with close friends but distant with everyone else.

Individuals with Mercury in Aquarius have an unusual sense of humor; not everyone can understand it. They don't like planning things and prefer to improvise. Their mind is objective: they can see and accept other's point of view. They are able to do several things simultaneously. Generally, they don't like to be in the center of attention.

In the worst-case scenario, these people can be unreliable, too scattered, lacking focus and easily forgetting their promises.

Mercury in Pisces

Mercury here isn't logical but intuitive. You could try hard to prove something practical to him, but it is normal for him to reply: "I don't feel like that". The minds of people with Mercury in Pisces are imaginative, sensitive and receptive. They usually think not in words but in images. It might take a long time for their ideas to take shape. They can be pretty indecisive.

Individuals with this Mercury's position are transmitters of any kind of information (they don't filter it). The first information they acquire on a subject is very important: it is difficult for them to switch over. They don't know how to defend their point of view, making it hard for them to speak sometimes; although, in a friendly environment they can be good narrators. People with Mercury in Pisces are not very sociable; they can be shy and low in self-confidence. Because they are able to feel others almost telepathically, they can talk to everyone in one's own language.

Teachers might complain about absent-mindedness concerning these children. Also, these people sometimes replace thinking with feelings. They can be confused, impractical and forgetful.

This Mercury's position can be beneficial for the occupations that require thinking in images, like painters, graphic designers, filmmakers and actors.

8

Dispositors' Chains and Four Key Planets

I call this chapter Dispositors' Chains, so it won't be confused with the Dispositors' Tree. Generally, we are talking about the same technique but using a different approach. A dispositor refers to a planet that rules the sign. For example, Sagittarius is the realm for Jupiter; Jupiter rules this sign: he is Sagittarius' dispositor. If there is any planet located in Sagittarius, Jupiter will have a significant influence over this planet.

First, I think I should explain the difference between the two techniques. The chart for the Dispositor's Tree looks like the diagram below::

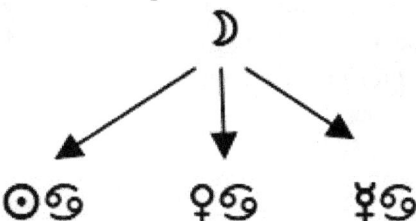

It means that there are three planets in Cancer and, since the Moon rules Cancer, she is the dispositor for the Sun, Venus and Mercury. Her influence on those planets is substantial.

For the Dispositors' Chain we'll have a reversed picture.

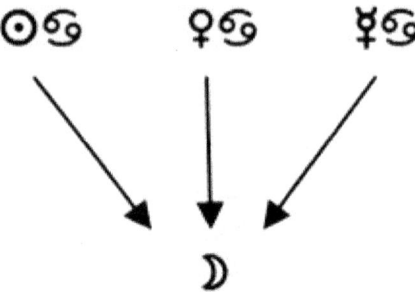

The Moon is still the dispositor. The idea here is that all these planets in the Moon's sign are increasing the Moon's significance. We'll need this type of chain in order to find four key planets that can be extremely important in analyzing someone's personality. This technique has been created in the Avestan School of Astrology in Russia. I have been using it for more than thirty years of my practice and found it very accurate and enlightening.

These key planets, called Atlas, Antaeus, Sisyphus and Icarus, represent our strongest and weakest personal trends on psychological and energy levels. Knowing these planets can be very useful in understanding own character and those of others. In order to find the mentioned planets, we will have to build planetary chains according to their realm, exaltation, detriment and fall. This is also the difference with the Dispositors' Tree method, since we use all four special planetary placements, not just one home sign.

The table below will be helpful for building chains. You can see that Chiron and Proserpina found their places there. If you don't want to use them, they can be omitted. For Pisces, Aquarius and Scorpio, we will use both rulers. Chiron rules Libra together with Venus.

	Realm	Exaltation	Detriment	Fall
Aries	Mars	Sun	Venus, Chiron	Saturn
Taurus	Venus	Moon	Mars, Pluto	Uranus
Gemini	Mercury	Proserpina	Jupiter	Chiron
Cancer	Moon	Jupiter	Saturn	Mars
Leo	Sun	Pluto	Saturn, Uranus	Neptune
Virgo	Mercury, Proserpina	Mercury	Jupiter, Neptune	Venus
Libra	Venus, Chiron	Saturn	Mars	Sun
Scorpio	Mars, Pluto	Uranus	Venus	Moon
Sagittarius	Jupiter	Chiron	Mercury	Proserpina
Capricorn	Saturn	Mars	Moon	Jupiter
Aquarius	Saturn, Uranus	Neptune	Sun	Pluto
Pisces	Jupiter, Neptune	Venus	Mercury, Proserpina	Mercury

Realm chains. Atlas

Let's start building Dispositors' Chains using planets in their homes. As an example, I'd like to take Justin Trudeau's (the 23rd Canadian Prime Minister) chart (Figure 8).

I usually begin building chains with the Sun. You can use any other planet if you wish. Justin's Sun is in Capricorn, ruled by Saturn; Saturn is in Gemini, ruled by Mercury. Mercury's location is in Sagittarius. Jupiter's realm is in Sagittarius and he is positioned in the same sign. There is another planet in Sagittarius, Neptune: draw an arrow from Neptune to

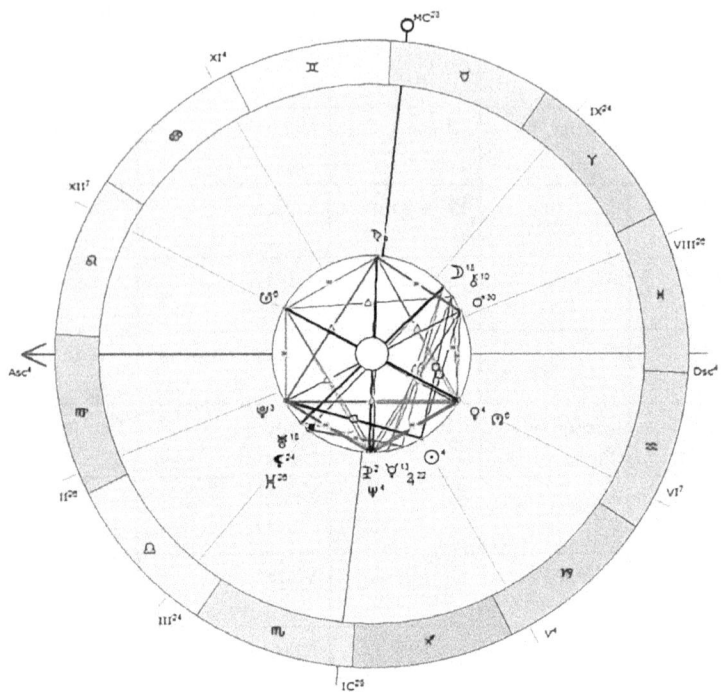

*Figure 8. Justin Trudeau, December 25, 1971, 21:27 GMT -5
Ottowa, Ontario, Canada*

☉ 3 ♑ 39'	♄ 0 ♊ 46' ℞	⚷ 23 ♎ 16'
☽ 17 ♈ 17'	♅ 17 ♎ 57'	⚴ 1 ♐ 26'
☿ 12 ♐ 44'	♆ 3 ♐ 54'	⚵ 25 ♎ 10'
♀ 3 ♒ 30'	♇ 2 ♎ 02'	⚶ 9 ♈ 22'
♂ 29 ♓ 35'	☊ 05 ♒ 40'	Asc 3 ♍ 35'
♃ 21 ♐ 02'	☋ 05 ♌ 40'	Mc 27 ♉ 17'

Jupiter. The second Jupiter's realm is in Pisces, where we can find Mars: draw two arrows to Jupiter and Neptune (Neptune's realm is Pisces).

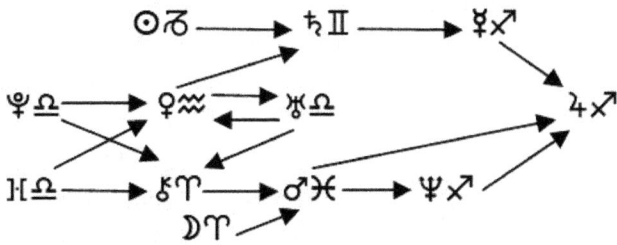

Chain 1. Realms. Justin Trudeau

Mars's home is in Aries and Scorpio. There is no one in Scorpio, but two planets in Aries: the Moon and Chiron. Chiron's realm is in Libra (as well as Venus'). There are three planets in Libra: Uranus, Pluto and Proserpina. We'll draw arrows from them to both Venus and Chiron. Venus is in Aquarius, which is home to Uranus and Saturn. You should notice that Venus and Uranus have two arrows pointed towards each other. This position is called mutual reception. We'll talk about it a bit later.

When we count all planets in the chain, we should get the number 12 – if using Chiron and Proserpina (that's how we know that no one is missing). The key planet for this chain is the one at the end, Jupiter. He has three arrows pointing at him and, because Jupiter is in his own realm, he is not subordinated to anyone. He is the true Atlas.

In Greek mythology Atlas was one of the Titans who participated in the war with the Olympian gods. The war was lost by the Titans and, as a punishment; Atlas was condemned to forever hold the heavens on his shoulders on the Western side of the Earth.

Atlas-planet in one's horoscope shows the backbone of the personality. It is precisely the planet which gives the confidence and the opportunity for the person to feel himself as individuality different from others. Atlas determines deep abilities and talents, although this planet sometimes shows itself in a latent form or – secretly – mainly on the inner level. If Atlas has a strong position (in his own realm or in the sign of exaltation), he can be pretty visible.

In Trudeau's chart Atlas – Jupiter is in a very strong position, in his realm, and it is definitely visible. The core of Justin's personality is authority, social justice and following deeply believed principals. In astrology, Jupiter also symbolizes expansion and success. Trudeau needed authority figures for his growth, and he was lucky in this regard: he had an example in his powerful father (also a Prime Minister). Being a figure of authority or just a person respected by others is important for people with Jupiter as an Atlas. Getting a good education is also a significant thing for this position. If Atlas is located in a sign where he isn't strong, he might not be able to realize his dreams, and dreams of power would be all that are left.

Let's look at another example. Barack Obama's (the 44th President of the United States) chart is shown in Figure 5 (in Chapter One). I don't use Proserpina in this chain because she doesn't play any significant role in this case and only makes the picture crowded.

We can see that this realms' chain also has a key planet at the end of the chain. This planet is the Sun and that is no surprise since Obama is a Leo. He also has two more planets in Leo: Mercury and Uranus, which make this sign stronger. The Sun is the true Atlas. This kind of Atlas makes a person bright, noticeable, and creative. All these qualities were given to Barack at birth, as a gift. The same as Trudeau had the gift of Jupiter located in his own realm. Both the Sun and Jupiter as an Atlas can make a person pretty ambitious. In those two cases the ambitions have been fulfilled. Atlas also shows what gives confidence. For Obama, he was supposed to just have it, without proving anything. However, a square aspect from Neptune to the Sun makes the situation more difficult and brings doubts to the personality. Barack spent a lot of his youth searching for his true identity. Therefore, it is necessary to analyse the whole chart before coming to a conclusion.

Sometimes it isn't easy to find the key planet. Look at the Dispositors' Chain for Audrey Hepburn (her chart – Figure 7 in Chapter Two).

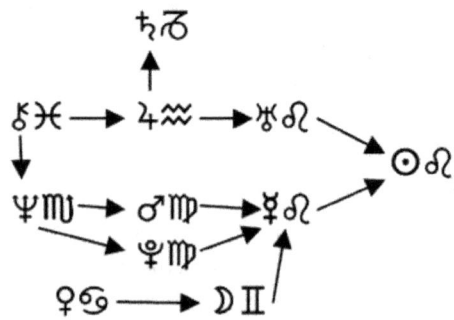

Chain 2. Realms. Barack Obama

There is no final planet in this chain. Neptune could be the one, but he is in Leo so we must point an arrow to the Sun (that is a Leo's ruler). So, Neptune is not the planet that collects everybody's energy. In this case the role of Atlas will be played by a planet with the greatest number of connections. Venus has four arrows directed towards her: from the Sun, Jupiter, Chiron and Proserpina. No other planet has even three connections. Venus is the Atlas for Audrey.

Venus is the planet of love and beauty. Audrey was definitely lovely and beautiful. However, Venus is in Aries, the sign of her detriment. Be-

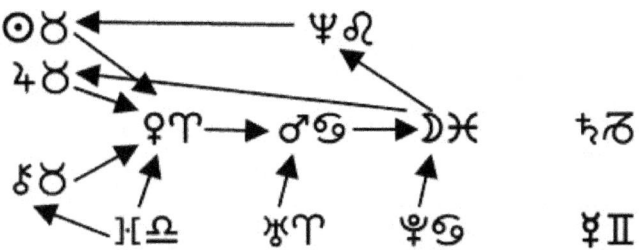

Chain 3. Realms. Audrey Hepburn

ing in this weak position, she can't be the true Atlas. In addition, Mars, which is the dispositor of Venus, forms a square aspect to her. This might not give the Venus harmony she deserved. These difficult indexes can also add to problems with childbirth (Audrey had a few miscarriages).

However, with regard of talent, Venus was very bright and noticeable (partially thanks to the same Mars). Hepburn's first career was in ballet (related to Venus and Mercury). A wonderful trine aspect from Neptune to Venus helped in her success in movies.

As you may notice, there are two planets that are not included in the chain: Saturn in Capricorn and Mercury in Gemini. These planets are in their homes and are not connected to other planets. These planets, not included in the chain, are referred to as being "switched off". It is believed in my astrological school that the "switched off" planet is an unpredictable planet that can have impressive and still-untouched reserves. However, since it is not fully participating in planetary interconnections, it is extremely difficult for a person to access those reserves. Saturn and Mercury are responsible for the rational element in our personality. For

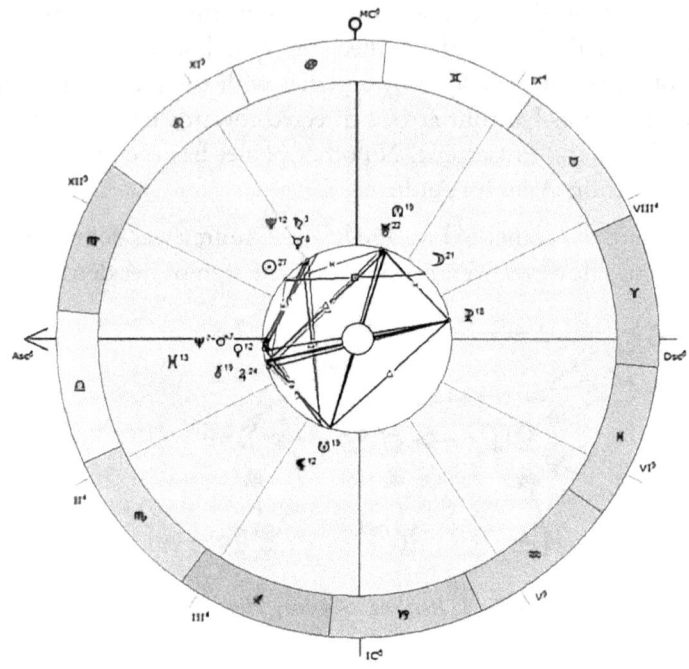

Figure 9. Bill Clinton, August 19, 1946, 8:51 GMT -6
Hope, Arkansas

☉ 3 ♑ 39'	♄ 0 ♊ 46' ℞	⚷ 23 ♎ 16'
☽ 17 ♈ 17'	♅ 17 ♎ 57'	⚴ 1 ♐ 26'
☿ 12 ♐ 44'	♆ 3 ♐ 54'	]·[25 ♎ 10'
♀ 3 ♒ 30'	♇ 2 ♎ 02'	⚸ 9 ♈ 22'
♂ 29 ♓ 35'	☊ 05 ♒ 40'	Asc 3 ♍ 35'
♃ 21 ♐ 02'	☋ 05 ♌ 40'	Mc 27 ♉ 17'

Hepburn they stayed alone, on the side, making her personality more spontaneous and intuitive than sensible and rational. Venus in Aries gives the tendency to love at first sight, and Saturn with Mercury definitely

Chain 4. Realms. Bill Clinton

is not helping here with sensibility. However, a developed and mindful person is able to take advantage of "switched off" planets.

Be aware that sometimes it is impossible to determine the Atlas (or some other key planets). As an example of this case, let's look at Bill Clinton's chart (Figure 9).

Clinton has two stelliums in Leo and Libra. A stellium is a gathering of more than three planets in one sign. There are just two planets located in other signs in his chart.

In this case we have two chains. It is possible to have two Atlases. We still shall find which one has a better position, and this planet would be the true Atlas. However, in this particular case, both the Sun and Venus (which has more arrows that Chiron) are in their realms. There is basically no Atlas. According to these chains, Bill Clinton divided his life between his own self-development and showing his best, and love affairs and, possibly, entertainment. Libra is also the sign of justice, and Clinton has done a lot of humanitarian work in his life. Leo generally is a very sincere sign; so, I believe, is Bill Clinton. However, this split in his chart may have prevented him from achieving his full potential.

Exaltation Chains. Antaeus

For these chains we'll need to look at the above table for the signs of exaltation. A planet in exaltation is on its throne, the highest possible place. The realms are also very positive, since planets feel so comfortable in their homes. But planets in exaltation are in an even stronger position. After constructing this chain, we can find the Antaeus planet. This planet will show the deep source of personal strength, the source a person can derive his energy from.

There is a difference between Atlas and Antaeus. They are both positive planets, but Atlas should be taken into consideration from the psychological point of view and Antaeus from the energy one.

In Greek mythology, Antaeus was the son of Poseidon and Gaia. Looks like this guy definitely needed an anger management course. He challenged a lot of people to fight and never lost. His secret was: whenever he got tired, he just needed to touch the earth (his mother) and he would regain all his strength. This changed when he met Heracles. Heracles discovered Antaeus' secret and, being a strong dude himself, lifted his opponent and didn't let him touch the ground. That's how Antaeus was defeated.

As the first example, let's look again at Barack Obama's chart. He has a few planets in Leo; we'll start with them.

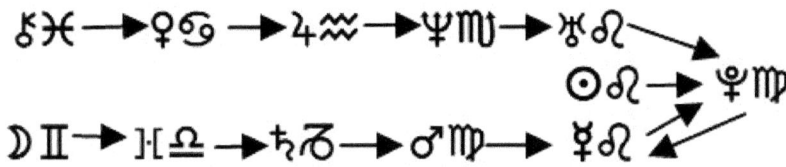

Chain 5. Exaltations. Barack Obama

The planet that exalts in Leo is Pluto. Draw three arrows to Pluto from the Sun, Mercury, and Uranus. Pluto is located in Virgo, which is Mercury's place of exaltation. Pluto and Mercury exchange arrows: they are in mutual reception through exaltation. There is one more planet in Virgo: Mars. It should also be connected with Mercury. You can try to finish this chain yourself. Exaltation chains are easier that those of realms because there is only one sign of exaltation for each planet.

We have two planets at the end of this chain, and they are in mutual reception. Mutual Reception happens when planets are dispositors for each other: this creates a strong connection between them. These planets support and supplement each other (on the psychological or energy level). They can even bring together the signs they are in. Reception can make a character richer and brighter or it can make it tangled.

In Obama's case, Pluto–Mercury in mutual reception is a nice occurrence. Mercury is responsible for speech and thinking and Pluto represents collective energy, the masses. This immediately shows that Barack

Obama should be an excellent public speaker. Because those two planets are also Antaeus' (the source of energy), being with people and talking to crowds will increase Obama's energy level. Neither Pluto nor Mercury is located in special signs, but their mutual support makes them stronger.

If we look at the planetary exaltation for Bill Clinton, we won't see any split chains. Actually, all planets will lead us directly to the true Antaeus: Pluto. Pluto is at the end of the chain and he is in his exalting sign, Leo. Clinton will gain energy being with people, the bigger the crowd the better. Bill doesn't have Obama's Pluto-Mercury reception but his

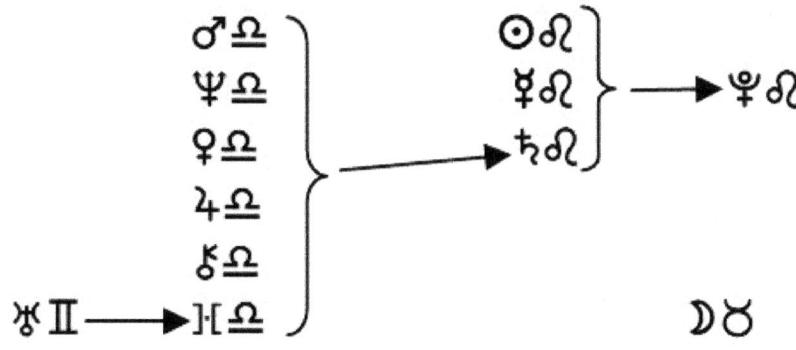

Chain 6. Exaltations. Bill Clinton

Mercury, positioned in Leo, clearly shows that he can be an enthusiastic speaker. Sometimes, when Pluto is in a negative position, a person who has him as Antaeus might find drive in extreme and dangerous situations. This doesn't concern Clinton since his Pluto is in a favorable position and doesn't have any stressful aspects.

There is the "switch off" planet in this chain: the Moon, located in the sign of its exaltation, Taurus. The position of the Moon is strong in the sign but she doesn't have any major aspects to other planets. This kind of planet is called an isolated planet. The Moon is also excluded from the energy-gaining chain. It could tell us that Clinton, for most of his life, wasn't aware of his emotions. His emotions could act as a time bomb.

It is also possible to have two exaltation chains. If we take Mother Teresa's chart (Figure 10), we can see exactly that.

There are two chains: one contains seven planets and ends at Mer-

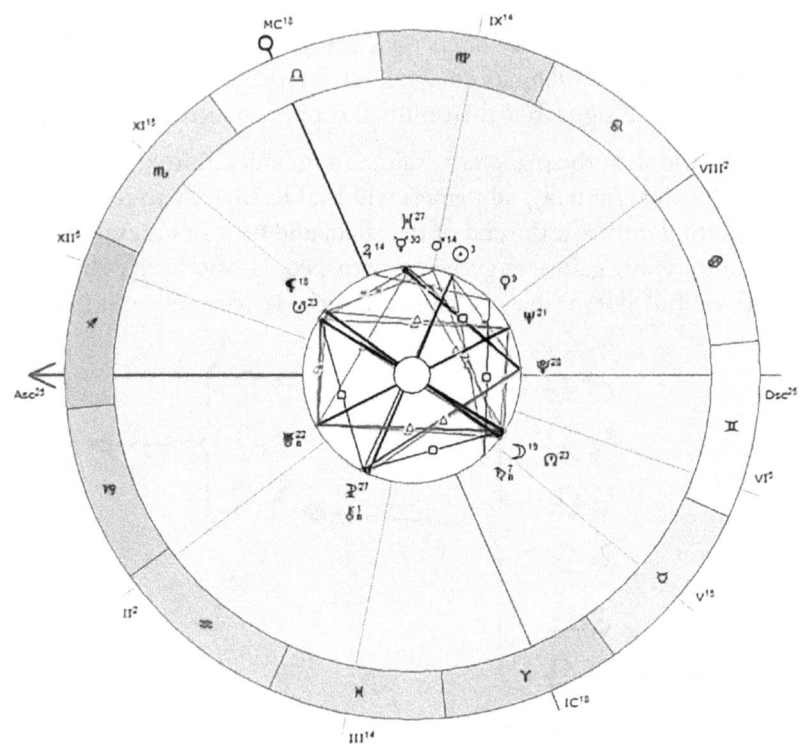

*Figure 10. Mother Teresa, August 26, 1910, 14:25 GMT +1
Skopje, Macedonia*

☉ 2 ♍ 25'	♄ 6 ♉ 32' ℞	⚷ 17 ♏ 43'
☽ 17 ♉ 37'	♅ 21 ♑ 47' ℞	⚴ 26 ♒ 39'
☿ 29 ♍ 12'	♆ 20 ♋ 37'	⊕ 26 ♍ 05'
♀ 8 ♌ 54'	♇ 27 ♊ 45'	⚸ 0 ♓ 08' ℞
♂ 13 ♍ 01'	☊ 22 ♉ 47'	Asc 24 ♐ 16'
♃ 13 ♎ 49'	☋ 22 ♏ 47'	Mc 18 ♎ 00'

cury; the other five planets lead to the Moon. Both are located in their exalting signs; neither Mercury nor the Moon is stronger. Here we have

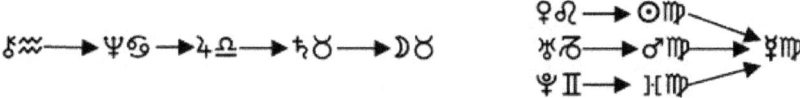

Chain 7. Exaltations. Mother Teresa

two Antaeuses. Mother Teresa was equally comfortable dealing with her emotions (the Moon) or her rational mind (Mercury).

Detriment Chains. Sisyphus

It is important to know our strong parts but, I believe, sometimes it is more important to be aware of our weak traits. Detriment and fall chains will show us the latter. Planets in their detriment signs are not comfortable. Detriment signs are in opposition with the realm ones. For example, one of Venus's realms is in Libra, the sign of balance and harmony. The sign of detriment will be Aries, which opposes Libra. The ruler of Aries is Mars with his active, impulsive and somewhat aggressive energy. It is a pretty uncomfortable place for Venus, who prefers peace, harmony and comfort.

The key planet for this type of chain is called Sisyphus. Sisyphus expresses the deepest personal psychological complex. In general, it is the source of all complexes. Our doubts, uncertainties, fears...they are all there. We have to work hard on the problematic Sisyphus planet; otherwise, it can get us into more trouble.

In Greek mythology, Sisyphus was the king of Corinth. He was known to be a very crafty, self-possessed, and deceitful man. He killed travellers and guests, which was considered a huge violation of law. Sisyphus even dared to play clever games with Zeus himself and other lesser gods. After his death as a punishment for his trickery and cruelty, he was made to roll a huge boulder up a steep hill. As soon as the boulder reached the top it would start rolling down and his fruitless labour had to start anew. Pointless and frustrating activities are now called Sisyphean.

As the first example, I'd like to look at the Detriment Chain for Indira Gandhi, India's first and only female Prime Minister (Figure 11). If we start with the Sun, we draw an arrow from him to Venus because Scorpio (Sun's sign) is the detriment place for Venus. Venus is in Capricorn, where the Moon is in detriment. The Moon is located in Capricorn

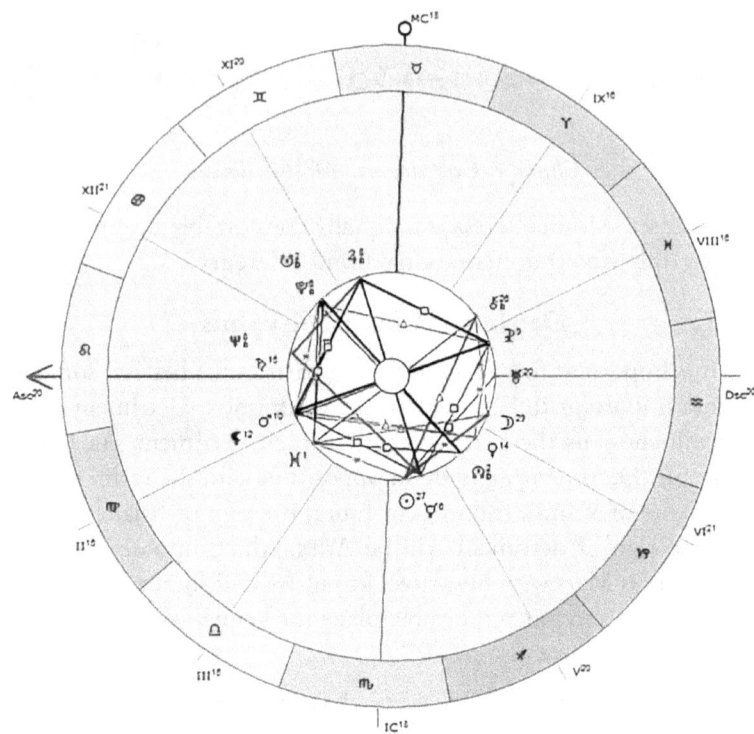

Figure 11. Indira Gandhi, November 19, 1917, 23:10 GMT +5:30 Allahabad, India

☉ 26 ♏ 50'	♄ 14 ♌ 30'	⚷ 11 ♍ 58'
☽ 28 ♍ 18'	♅ 19 ♒ 58'	♆ 8 ♓ 45'
☿ 5 ♐ 57'	♆ 7 ♌ 05' ℞	]·[0 ♎ 18'
♀ 13 ♑ 43'	♇ 5 ♋ 10'	⚸ 25 ♓ 33' ℞
♂ 9 ♍ 05'	☊ 1 ♑ 55' D	Asc 19 ♌ 52'
♃ 7 ♊ 43' ℞	☋ 1 ♋ 55' D	Mc 17 ♉ 30'

too, so this will be the end of this chain. Just to make sure it is right, we add the other nine planets. All the planets, except Mercury, lead to the

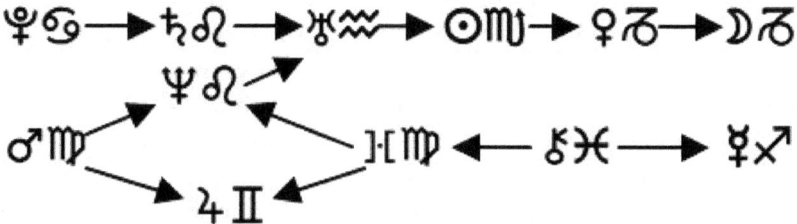

Chain 8. Detriments. Indira Gandhi

Moon. The Moon is the true Sisyphus since she is positioned in the sign of her detriment.

The Sisyphus planet represents our psychological issues, which always have roots in emotions. The Moon is the planet that is responsible for our emotions, making the problem even deeper. Capricorn is the sign where emotions are suppressed. It is extremely difficult for a person with this Moon to express her emotions freely. The Moon has a positive sextile aspect to the Sun, indicating that emotions are stable but not cancelling the issue of pushing emotional problems deep into the subconscious.

The Moon also represents the Mother figure. Indira Gandhi wanted to be the mother for her nation. In the beginning she was deeply loved by many, especially women whose rights Indira fought for. However, with the Sun in Scorpio and the Moon in Capricorn, her motherly love was not soft. Her "children" had to be obedient. If not, she would punish them. Also having a strong Capricorn in her chart added serious centralization of power during her governing years.

For the second example let's look at the chart of Marilyn Monroe (Figure 4 – Chapter One). We could see that there are two almost-separate chains, but they are united by Neptune. The key planets will be the Sun and Jupiter in mutual anti-reception. When planets are in each other's signs of detriment (or fall), we call this position anti-reception in my astrological school. Its energy is opposite from mutual reception: planets here don't support each other; on the contrary, they try to destroy each other. There is a negative energy that pushes them apart. They inhibit each other's functions and hinder personal growth. People with planets in anti-reception might have feelings of imbalance and even chaos in areas ruled by these planets.

Monroe's Sun is in Gemini, the detriment sign for Jupiter. Jupiter is in Aquarius, the Sun's detriment. These planets in anti-reception play the role of Sisyphus for Marilyn. In this case the Sun, that is self-esteem and independence, is in an unfortunate relationship with Jupiter, which represents authority and power figures. Being with powerful people was a substitute for personal confidence and created co-dependence. It looks like Marilyn needed relationships with authority figures to feel OK. However, it didn't work this way. Jupiter was destruction for her creative and confident self, not support. When Monroe thought that people didn't

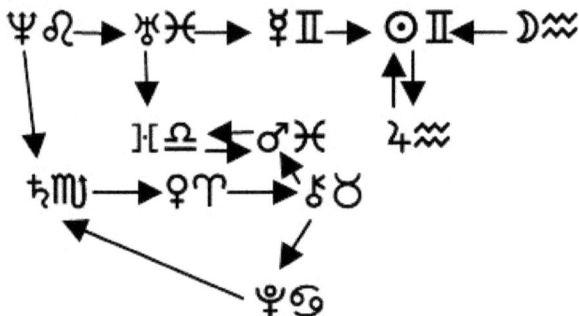

Chain 9. Detriments. Marilyn Monroe

desire her enough, her anxiety level would skyrocket. As compensation for her low self-esteem, Marilyn had to be highly noticeable.

In this chain we can also see another anti-reception between Mars and Proserpina. Those two also play a key role. In addition to deep inner changes, Proserpina is also responsible for our everyday life, the routine and small, sometimes annoying, details. It looks like Marilyn Monroe had no patience for that. She didn't want to spend any energy (Mars) on those small, "unnecessary" things. This planetary connection also shows that the feeling of being small and unnoticeable could be devastating for Marilyn's will power (Mars). This anti-reception though is much less important that Sisyphus' anti-reception.

Fall Chains. Icarus

The key planet of the chain, where we take into consideration planets in fall, is called Icarus. In Greek mythology Icarus was a son of master craftsman Daedalus, who was the creator of the Labyrinth on

Crete. Daedalus and his son had to escape urgently from the island. The master constructed two pairs of wings from feathers and wax. His father warned Icarus not to fly too close to the sun, but the youth didn't listen. Icarus flew higher and higher until the hot sun's rays melted the wax and he fell and drowned in the sea.

Icarus shows the weakest planet in one's chart from the energy point of view (Sisyphus has a relation with psychology only). Icarus is like a black hole draining energy. It clearly shows what we need to change in ourselves in order to avoid possible personal degradation. Since Icarus sucks up the energy from other planets in the chain, it needs close attention – the earlier in life the better.

Let's look at the fall chain for Bill Clinton. Since he has two stelliums in his chart, it is easy to determine the key planet. However, in this case we have two Icaruses connected by anti-reception: the Sun and Neptune. Neptune is in his fall in Leo where the Sun is located, and the Sun falls in Libra where Neptune is positioned. However, if we apply the rule that a planet can't be Sisyphus or Icarus if it is in the sign of its realm or exaltation, then we'll have to exclude the Sun. That leaves Neptune for the rule of Icarus.

Neptune here is bringing an issue with trust as well as wishful

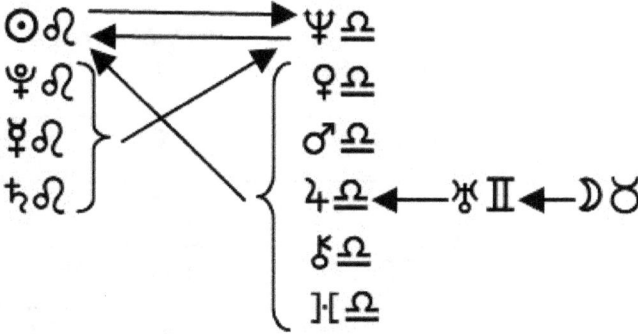

Chain 10. Falls. Bill Clinton

thinking. Clinton might have concerns about the sincerity of people towards him. If he believes that he's been deceived he'd lose a lot of energy. The same happens with suspicion. Sometimes people with Neptune-Icarus question the validity of facts and believe in something they wish to be true, but it is not. If someone has Neptune as an Icarus, this person

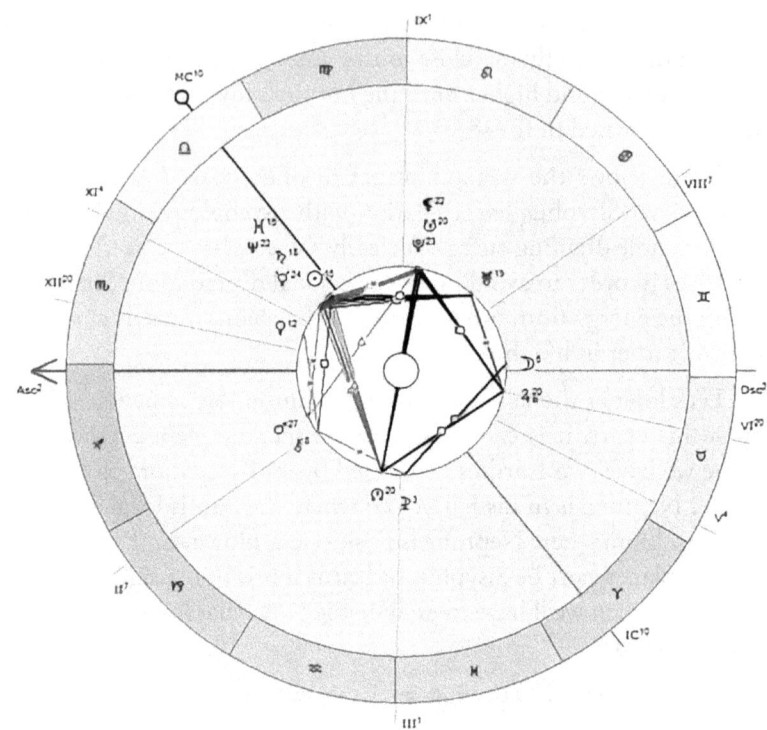

Figure 12. Vladimir Putin, October 7, 1952, 12:31 GMT +3
St Petersburg, Leningradskaja obl., Russia

☉ 26 ♏ 50'	♄ 14 ♌ 30'	⚷ 11 ♍ 58'
☽ 28 ♍ 18'	♅ 19 ♒ 58'	⚴ 8 ♓ 45'
☿ 5 ♐ 57'	♆ 7 ♌ 05' ℞	]·[0 ♎ 18'
♀ 13 ♑ 43'	♇ 5 ♋ 10'	⚸ 25 ♓ 33' ℞
♂ 9 ♍ 05'	☊ 1 ♑ 55' D	Asc 19 ♌ 52'
♃ 7 ♊ 43' ℞	☋ 1 ♋ 55' D	Mc 17 ♉ 30'

shouldn't ever take drugs.

Now let's consider the fall chain of the President\Tsar of Russia,

Vladimir Putin (Figure 12). It is clear that the Sun is at the end of the chain. Since the Sun is in Libra, the sign of fall, he is the true Icarus. This brings a deep issue with self-esteem. Putin needs constant admiration and reassurance not just as a person but also as a male. He needs to be different from others, higher and better. He might love flattery.

However, the Sun is on Midheaven (MC), which is a very strong position. We also have to compare the pair Antaeus – Icarus and see which one is stronger. Putin's Antaeus is Saturn, which is in the sign of his exaltation in Libra. Saturn is also in conjunction with the Sun. A very strong Antaeus shows that whatever complexes Icarus can be successfully dealt with. Putin's issues with the Sun are not noticeable on the surface; however, I believe that exactly those unresolved inner problems with Icarus-Sun made him start the war with Ukraine (and the entire world). His need to prove his greatness to all citizens of "his empire" made the majority of the world wish him dead.

I would now suggest taking the astrological chart of a certain person and looking through all dispositor's chains, trying to get the whole

Chain 11. Falls. Vladimir Putin

picture. Let this certain person be the 45th American President, Donald Trump, because he is a very colourful figure and has an interesting horoscope (Figure 13).

We'll begin with the planetary chain according to realms (Chain 12). You can see that this is a rather complicated one. However, it still leads us to two key planets with the most connections: Chiron and Venus. However, Venus has four arrows and Chiron just three. It looks like Venus should be playing the role of Atlas.

Venus is known as a planet of love, but it is also a very materialistic planet, responsible not only for love but, in addition, for money and luxury, indicating that Trump might be very attached to his comfort. Since in his chart Venus rules the tenth house (career, goals) and the

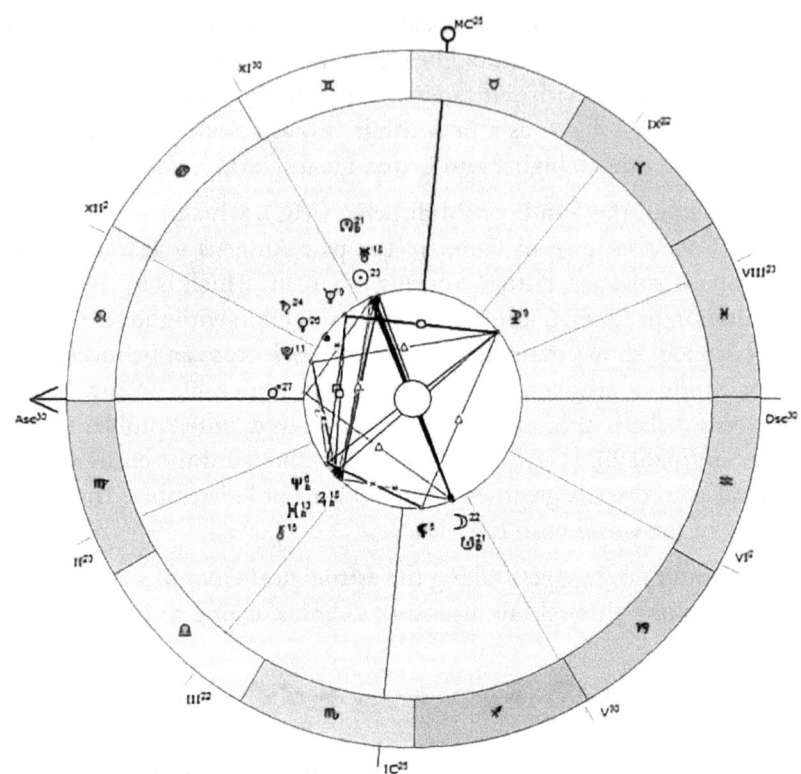

Figure 13. Donald Trump, June 14, 1946, 10:54 GMT -4
New York, New York, USA

☉ 26 ♏ 50'	♄ 14 ♌ 30'	⚷ 11 ♍ 58'
☽ 28 ♍ 18'	♅ 19 ♒ 58'	8 ♓ 45'
☿ 5 ♐ 57'	♆ 7 ♌ 05' ℞	⚴ 0 ♎ 18'
♀ 13 ♑ 43'	♇ 5 ♋ 10'	☋·[25 ♓ 33' ℞
♂ 9 ♍ 05'	☊ 1 ♑ 55' D	Asc 19 ♌ 52'
♃ 7 ♊ 43' ℞	☋ 1 ♋ 55' D	Mc 17 ♉ 30'

second house (money), as Atlas she represents more of finance/luxury/convenience than love. For his personal fulfilment Trump needs this area

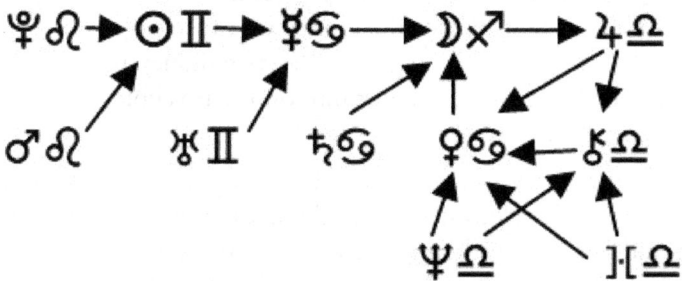

Chain 12. Realms. Donald Trump

to be secure.

Chain 13 shows the exaltation chain with the key Antaeus planet (the source of inner strength and energy). This chain leads us to the mutual reception between Jupiter and Saturn. Jupiter is in Saturn's sign of exaltation (Libra) and Saturn is in Jupiter's (Cancer). These two planets support each other. Trump's personal goals help in achieving power and authority and vice versa. There are two planets that are excluded from this chain: Pluto and Mars. Pluto is in his own sign of exaltation, Leo, and Mars is in the same sign and there are no planets in Capricorn, Mars' place of exaltation. When some planets (usually just one) are not connected to other planets in the chain, they don't participate in giving strength (or weakness – depending on the chain). It is interesting that for

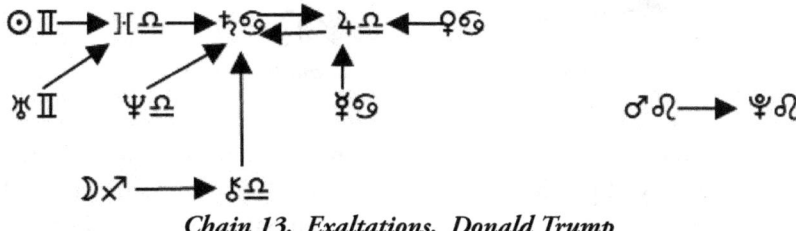

Chain 13. Exaltations. Donald Trump

Donald Trump, the planets that are related to energy (Mars to personal energy and Pluto to collective energy) are excluded.

If we look closer at two key planets of the exaltation chain, we notice that Saturn is in the sign of his own detriment, Cancer, and can't be the true Antaeus. This leaves only Jupiter as Antaeus. This means that Trump's natural source of energy comes from power, being an authoritative figure and an ideological leader. Jupiter is also related to big money, while Venus is responsible for the money we can actually touch and buy nice things with. It is interesting that those two money-related planets are in favour with Trump and support him on the psychological and energy levels.

It is time now to move from the strong to the weak points. On Chain 14 we see the detriment chain. Look carefully at this picture. Both Saturn and Mars have the biggest number of arrows – four. However, Saturn is at the end of the chain, so he will be Sisyphus in this example. Saturn is also in his detriment position in Cancer, meaning he is the true Sisyphus, removing him completely from the consideration of being one of the possible Antaeuses.

Saturn as Sisyphus brings psychological complexes with goal-management, self-values and self-confidence, feelings of isolation and various fears, especially a fear of loneliness. People with this kind of Saturn might need constant reassurance that they are special. We always need to look at

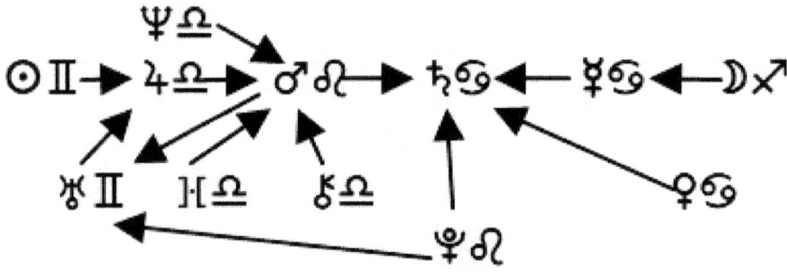

Chain 14. Detriments. Donald Trump

the pair Atlas – Sisyphus together; then it will be possible to see if there is a probability of psychological compensation. In Trump's case the Atlas is Venus which is not as strong as Saturn (but Saturn is strong in a negative way).

So, this suggests the possibility of compensation, but in what way? Saturn feels lonely and needs the love that Venus can provide. However, Venus' position is weaker than Saturn's. So, the collection of trophy wives might not help overall. Of course, Venus can provide the comfort of nice things but, since she is weaker, it would never be enough.

Now let's consider the last chain, for planets in fall (Chain 15). It is clear that the key planets at the end of the chain are the Sun and Chiron in mutual anti-reception. As has been mentioned, anti-reception has the opposite characteristics to mutual reception. Planets here are some sort of enemies, they don't support each other. This situation put Trump's personality into a very difficult position: Chiron here is against the Sun, the very spirit, and the driving force of the personality. In my astrological school, Chiron is responsible for compromise, duality and alternative, as well as balance, justice, and diplomacy. In the worst-case scenario, unkind Chiron can make a person very confused, insincere, prone to intrigues and manipulative. It suggests that the lower Chiron's characteristics, like duality, hypocrisy, and manipulation, are harmful for personal self-development and creative abilities. On the other side, the need to

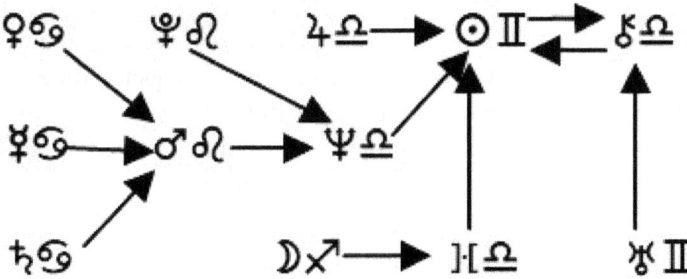

Chain 15. Falls. Donald Trump

look good (the Sun) might drive a person into lying and self-confusion.

Chiron is positioned in the sign of his realm, Libra. Because of that he can't be the true Icarus, which leaves the Sun for this role. If we think about the Sun – the luminary and the source of life – being a black hole sucking energy, it doesn't feel right. However, in Trump's case this is the situation he has to deal with. With the Sun as Icarus the weakest points on the energy level are doubts about one's creative abilities, self-worth, and uniqueness. The opposition between the Sun and the Moon in Trump's chart doesn't help either. It adds to the trouble with an absence of the feeling of being a complete person. People with this kind of Icarus planet can become very self-centered and attention-seeking.

When we compare Antaeus and Icarus, we can see that Jupiter and the Sun are not in their special signs (realm, exaltation, detriment or fall). These two planets belonging to the Fire element are located in the Air signs, so we can assume that they are equal in strength. Jupiter can somewhat help the Sun, but not much.

After analysing all chains, we can come to a conclusion. With two money-related planets, Jupiter and Venus, being strong and favourable on psychological and energy levels, Donald Trump draws energy and confidence from financial security as well as from having authority. This position encourages him to undertake actions in money-related fields and also in politics. However, politics comes second as a craving for more power. With a strong Chiron position and his unfortunate anti-reception with the Sun, we can't expect direct actions from Trump; he always leaves for himself a gate "to twist" the situation.

With two deficit planets, Saturn and the Sun, which are responsible for deep inner values and self-confidence, there might be a lot of doubts and insecurity if those issues haven't been corrected through inner work. Since Atlas/Antaeus are of almost the same strength as Sisyphus/Icarus, there is a slight chance for compensation of psychological deficiencies. How well it works you can judge yourself.

If you are a psychologist with skills in astrology, or an astrologer with skills in psychology, you might decide to use this technique in your practice. Taking into consideration that life events depend on the person's character, we may find that it is our mission to help a client in sorting out problems indicated in his chart. Sisyphus and Icarus attract the most attention in this regard. Both of these planets are weak spots in a human's personality, but they require totally different approaches. For example, if Mars acts as Sisyphus, it clearly means the complex of will, passivity, and inner uncertainty in one's own personal forces; an inability or unwillingness to insist on her or his opinion. It might be a deep feeling of cowardice. This is just the psychological complex, and it could be cured by the methods of psychotherapy. It is important to make the Atlas planet stronger. After reinforcing the backbone of the personality, it is much easier to compensate for the complexes.

However, if Mars acts as Icarus, the situation becomes more complicated. We have to deal not with psychology only, but with the energy aspect as well. The person with Mars – Icarus will not be a coward; he or she could have a strong will, but there will be some anxiety in his/her character regarding the Mars issues. This person could apprehend that he is not able to protect himself, and his relations, from negative circumstances (the sign of Zodiac where Mars is situated will show the sphere of concern). Therefore, this person will be constantly busy thinking over possible dangerous situations and even searching for non-existent enemies. Naturally, it happens with a large loss of energy. Since the person with Mars-Icarus usually goes in circles thinking about the same concerns, the loss of energy is constant. In the case of Icarus, it is necessary to find another way to explain to the client the source of the problem. Sometimes methods of psychotherapy are not enough. The main method can be the constant tracing of the "cyclic" thoughts and the immediate switching over. Being aware of what is going on is super important. If the client is familiar with energy work, some methods of healing may be helpful. And, of course, while working with Icarus we should take into consideration the Antaeus planet for the finding energy recourses and hopefully reinforcing them.

It is not my intention to give a detailed explanation of planets as four key points. It is easy to find the descriptions of ten of them (if you don't know it already) and just use your imagination. However, two planets that are unknown or have a different meaning in Western astrology need to be explained more thoroughly. I am talking about Proserpina and Chiron. They rarely play the role of key planets but if you happen to have them as Atlas etc., I will give more information.

Proserpina

Proserpina as Atlas is a very rare occurrence, possible only when there are a lot of planets in Virgo (where she rules with Mercury) and no planets in Gemini (Mercury's realm), otherwise, Mercury will outnumber Proserpina. The strengths Proserpina brings in this position are an ability to calculate everything (which doesn't leave space for spontaneous actions), a good detail-oriented mind and, in the best-case scenario, the ability to bring about total inner transformation.

Proserpina as Antaeus (possible with a lot of planets in Gemini) allows drawing energy from detailed plans that have been carefully thought through: the more organized the day is, the better a person feels. This gives him some sense of security. Those people usually don't like surprises, preferring everything be planned. They might even find joy in well-done, everyday routine. However, people with Antaeus-Proserpina can be unpredictable. Others might be used to them as they've been for years, and suddenly they can turn out to be somebody completely different.

Proserpina in the positions of Sisyphus and Icarus might not be visible at first sight. What drives those people nuts is the thought that they are just a small screw in a big machine. They need to feel some sort of self-importance. Usually they are capable of seeing the big picture and this can be overwhelming for them. They generally hate small details, preferring to contemplate grand tasks and theoretical ideas. It may be pretty difficult for them to be practical.

Chiron

Atlas-Chiron, first of all, brings an ability and ease of making choices to the personality. These people can weigh all the pros and cons to find a balanced decision. In the best-case scenario, their inner core is based on unbiased views and justice. They know how to compromise properly. People with this Atlas like to think everything through and are never in a rush, so don't expect quick decisions from them! However, you can be sure that they will look for alternatives.

Chiron as Antaeus draws energy from comfortable and peaceful situations. These people don't feel well in a stressful environment; they avoid it at any cost. They also don't like to do what they are told: they need to be able to choose.

Individuals with Chiron playing a role of Sisyphus might be easily confused. They don't know how to choose from multiple alternatives; they want things to be straight and clear. Sometimes they have no idea what diplomacy is about. In the worst-case scenario, they mix up concepts of good and evil.

It is extremely difficult for people with Chiron-Icarus to make choices. They try postponing making decisions as long as possible. Those individuals can't function properly in unclear or ambivalent situations. Parents of children with this Icarus should never make choices for their kids. Starting from a young age they should teach them how to make wise choices and not avoid them.

9

Rising Planets

I've decided to include this chapter to the AstroPsychology book because of the importance of rising planets (planets on ASC) for the personal character. Not so many people have planets on Ascendant but, if they do, the rising planet adds significant traits that can't go unnoticed. In order to figure out if there are rising planets in a personal chart, one has to know the exact time of birth. If it is known and the degree of ASC seems accurate, then look for the planetary glyphs close to ASC. The orb for the conjunction with the Ascendant is 10 degrees for the first house and five degrees for the twelfth house.

The importance of these planets comes from the fact that at the moment of one's birth they were rising above the horizon. This fact makes specific planets extra bright and prominent in life and character. If the rising planet doesn't have strong dignities, its characteristics might not be visible right away but they will show themselves with age.

The Sun on ASC

If you have a rising Sun in your chart, meaning that you were born on sunrise, it makes you a bit of a Leo with all its consequences.

The Sun makes a person bright, noticeable, generous and very creative. People with the rising Sun are very active and enthusiastic, always on a go and encourage others into their activities. They are attractive and are usually surrounded by a fair number of admirers. They are independent, have a lot of energy (provided by the Sun) and don't keep their opinions to themselves.

In the worst–case scenario, people with this shining Sun can become egocentric, vain, selfish and arrogant. Their attention to people isn't real but superficial, just for the purpose to impress. They usually don't admit their shortcomings.

Rising Moon

If you have the Moon on Ascendant, you might be struggling with the weight. This one of the unwanted "gifts" that rising Moon gives. People, who have it, are usually not heavy but somewhat round. I met a few women with the Moon on ASC who had beautiful, voluptuous, womanly shapes… but couldn't accept them. In this particular case, accepting is the best thing that can be done.

Other Moon's gifts are intuition, romantics, sensitivity, dreams and artistic abilities. The personality of these people forms under the influence of emotions. Their moods are pretty changeable. They are very dependable on the emotional comfort. The rising Moon can be found in horoscopes of actors, poets, artists and musicians.

Some people with this Moon can be extremely moody, capricious, needy, lying and don't know what they actually want. Some of them may resemble spoiled children.

Mercury on ASC

In this case it is the intellect that is the most important. Contacts and information are needed for forming personality. Usually people with rising Mercury have rational mind and fast thinking. They are able swiftly switch from subject to subject. They are pretty sociable and don't like being alone. This position is positive for writers, journalists, preachers and sometimes politicians. For example, Ernest Hemingway had Mercury rising in Leo. George W Bush and Keanu Reeves also have rising Mercury; however, they both have more than one rising planet. We'll talk about multiple rising planets at the end of this chapter.

If Mercury has stressful aspects, he might give talkativeness, extra coolness and lack of emotions. These people can talk about everything and nothing.

Rising Venus

Having Venus on the ASC is excellent for females. She doesn't bring good looks only but also gives person sophistication, elegance, style, refinement, softness and a good artistic taste. Males will have the same excellent qualities but some of them might look a bit feminine. People with this Venus take serious care about their appearance. They are very attractive and like to charm. They are generally well-balanced people, patient and with good manners.

The typical chart with Venus rising is the chart of Angelina Jolie. You can see it in Chapter One. Her Venus in Cancer definitely gives Angelina her looks but it didn't provide patience and a tendency to compromise, which isn't a surprise with her numerous planets in Aries.

Generally people with Venus on the ASC don't like working; they feel better when they can lead a lazy life. Sometimes they are too sweet, mincing and unnatural. They need other people to love them.

There are a lot of people with rising Venus working in the beauty industry.

Mars on ASC

This personality forms under the influence of various fights and challenges. These people are competitive, impulsive and independent. The best of them are very honest but there is also aggressiveness and a big lack of diplomacy in them. The worst of them are rude, hot-tempered, inconsistent and insolent.

People with rising Mars like being leaders; however, their actions are often rash, they don't have time to think about consequences. The latter might not be true for those who have strong Mercury and Saturn. Individuals with Mars on ASC often interfere into lives of others without asking first. Their usual excuse is: "I want the best for you", meaning "I know better".

There are many world leaders among those with rising Mars: Donald Trump, Hannibal, Bolivar, Admiral Nelson. Bill Clinton also has

Mars on ASC but it is accompanied by rising Neptune and Venus which shows a completely different picture.

Rising Jupiter

Here Jupiter gives confidence and optimism as well as a gift of persuasion. In appearance rising Jupiter usually gives pretty high forehead, and, in the worst-case scenario, a bit of heaviness in the body constitution.

People with Jupiter on ASC can be very different but they always project some kind of authority outside. The worst on them can be arrogant (right up to megalomania), close-minded, overly conservative, boastful and like to show off. The best of them are generous, seriously concerned about welfare of others and open-minded.

There are a lot of personalities of politicians, teachers, spiritual leaders and missionaries. Michael Gorbachov has Jupiter on ASC in his natal chart.

Saturn on ASC

Well, you might not like some traits of Saturn but there is always one adventure: it is very difficult to get fat for people with this kind of horoscope.

Others might see people with Saturn rising as a bit gloomy, distant, strict and prudish, even arrogant. However, this is only a mask. Behind the façade you can find a shy and overwhelmed with responsibilities personality. People with Saturn on ASC are serious, reliable, decent and responsible. They don't talk much and don't like empty conversations. If they are around shallow and talkative people, they'll just make themselves disappear.

A person with Saturn on ASC can be the kindest soul on the Earth but others will always feel distance (or barrier) between them. People with this position of Saturn learn from their experience and, if this life experience doesn't make them wiser, it makes them tougher.

In the worst-case scenario, a person with Saturn rising might turn into a pessimist who is angry and disappointed at the whole world and see all things from the negative side only. This person also can be very slow in development and difficult in communication.

Personalities with Saturn on ASC: Margaret Thatcher, Indira Gandhi, Dante Alighieri.

Rising Uranus

If Uranus is strong, these people are very unusual, unpredictable, interesting and talented. They have an excellent intuition. Uranus gives abilities in astrology and fortune telling. They also are reformers and can be ahead of their time. There are also a lot of scientists and inventors among them.

Individuals with Uranus rising are never conservative, value their freedom a lot, have fast reactions and often are an enigma to others.

If Uranus doesn't have a good status, he can give nervous exhaustion, adventurism and anarchism. Being around these people might not be easy.

Personalities with rising Uranus: Franklin D Roosevelt, Hilary Clinton, Edgar Cayce – "The Sleeping Prophet" and Heinrich Himmler.

Neptune on ASC

This is a very tricky planet to have on ASC. People with rising Neptune have interesting eyes, often very beautiful, and it sometimes seems as though those eyes look inside, not outside.

People with Neptune rising can be big idealists with an extrasensory perception. A lot of their actions are based on a subconscious side of personality and intuition. They can be mystics, artists, writers of fantasy books and musicians. They are able of feeling the higher harmony.

However, in the worst-case scenario, the outcome might be completely different: individuals with Neptune on Ascendant may be born liars. They will lie not only to others but to themselves as well. This is their way of living. They create their own reality and believe in it. They can't see the pattern of causes and consequences. Sometimes they like to play being a mysterious personality. If things go really bad, they can have manias: claustrophobia, acrophobia and persecution mania.

Personalities with Neptune rising: Johannes Kepler, Marilyn Monroe, Paris Hilton.

Rising Pluto

Pluto gives an amazingly strong energy to a person if he is on the rising in a personal chart. It is up to the person to use it in the right way. Often infants with rising Pluto have a very intense stare, like they are not little and already know a lot of things.

Sometimes it seems that these people have limitless recourses which they often direct to the collective processes in order to improve lives of themselves and others. Their energy is not aggressive like Mars's but very intense to the point of being "pushy". They are very active and involve others into their undertakings. For some individuals their influence on people can be even magical. There are a lot of leaders of revolutions with this strong Pluto. People with Pluto on ASC might act like an avalanche; they are confident, strong-willed and sometimes reckless (but have excellent survival skills). They can be very attractive but on the edge of fear.

If Pluto has a negative status or challenging aspects, this person might be extra-stubborn, despotic and cruel, at times capable of turning the lives of others into chaos.

As you understand, people with rising Pluto might be of the opposite polarities. For example, Mother Teresa and Pol Pot (a Cambodian dictator): they both had Pluto on Ascendant.

Chiron on ASC

Since Chiron can see two sides of things, he makes a person diplomatic, just and peace-loving. Chiron is always ready for a compromise. Because he loves justice, he tries to find the best solution suitable for everyone.

The character of a person with rising Chiron is very changeable. Different people can have very different opinions about him. He/she changes depending on the situation or environment. That's why individuals with Chiron rising can be excellent actors. Generally, they are easy people to be around: sociable and with good sense of humor. However, sometimes a question about their sincerity might arise…

In the worst-case scenario, life is just a game for them where they never play the real themselves. This is a chameleon type of person, which always uses his adaptability for his own gain.

Rising Proserpina

Being a planet of deep inner changes, Proserpina gives a chance of total transformation. At the certain point in life, when Proserpina becomes activated by transits or progressions, a person with this planet on ASC can be totally transformed into a new self, including one's appearance. Sometimes their life is so "rich" that it is enough for two – three lives.

People with rising Proserpina are perfectionists. They have excellent survival skills. If Proserpina is strong, they might have unusual abilities.

They also can have fixation on small details and be hypercritical. It may happen that they place their life under the command of cold and calculating mind and stop looking human. A robotic kind of existence...

People with Proserpina on ASC are very rarely tall. Some of them can have different-colored eyes. It seems to me that Tyrion Lanister from Game of Thrones could have rising Proserpina. Among real people I managed to find only one person with this position: Paul Gauguin, a famous artist.

Moon Nodes on ASC

Moon nodes don't give specific traits that planets can give. Nodes only put a focus on personality or, the opposite, make it vague. Rising North node makes an impression of a person brighter and much more noticeable. Rising South node, on the contrary, brings the point when even the most impressive personality might go unnoticeable and unrecognized. In the worst-case scenario, this person might look like "a grey mouse" even with the great potential. People with the South Moon node on ASC need others for the personal development, especially a partner.

If you noticed I always talk about both good outcome and the worst-case scenario. Planets manifest their good or not so good qualities depending on their status. The status depends on the position in signs and houses, and aspects toward planets. If you are a beginner, you might not figure out the planetary dignities; you'll need somebody more experienced.

Sometimes there is more than one planet on the ASC. These cases are complicated and need special attention. Let's take Bill Clinton's chart as an example (Figure 9 – Chapter Eight). He has Mars on Ascendant but Mars has an exact conjunction with Neptune. Venus is also rising after them. Neptune and Venus make Mars much softer, and this personality won't be as close as aggressive as it could be with only Mars rising. Mars and Neptune show that Clinton always believed in what he was doing. These three planets on ASC also made sure that his love affairs would go public.

George W Bush has rising Mercury and Pluto. Pluto is in Leo there and in very favorable aspects, and he supports Mercury, which gave Bush a great ability in talking and charming the public.

Keanu Reeves has Pluto, Uranus and Mercury conjunct the Sun, rising. This gave him a powerful, unpredictable, smart and a bit mysterious personality. When planets are in groups they always should be analyzed together.

10

A Scout Planet

A Scout is the closest Oriental planet to the Sun, and rises before the Sun. In some sources it is mentioned as a Guiding planet which determines the manifestation of personal qualities. In my astrological school a Scout planet is called Doryphoros (an armor-bearer), as it has been called in ancient astrology. The Doryphoros shows the direction of realization of a person's creative energy, playing a significant role in finding personal talents and abilities and used in vocational astrology.

It is especially important to identify a Scout planet in a child's chart because it will show what is important for their personal development. A Scout helps in awareness of "self".

It is not difficult to find the Scout planet in your chart. If you turn your chart so that the Sun is on top, then the closest planet to the right of the Sun will be the Scout. This is true of charts composed counterclockwise, as is common in North America. In my astrological school we do the chart clockwise, in which case we need to look at the closest planet to the Sun from the left side.

Let's look at the example of Van Gogh's chart (Figure 2). The first

Oriental planet is Venus. Having Venus as the Scout is very beneficial for an artist. The Scout planet for Angelina Jolie is Chiron (Figure 3). You could see both the White Moon and a Moon Node between the Sun and Chiron. We don't take fictitious planets into consideration regarding a Scout. The Scout planet for Barack Obama (Figure 5) will be Mercury.

The closer the Doryphoros is to the Sun, the earlier a person discovers their abilities and talents, making the path to understanding oneself easier. If the Scout is in conjunction with the Sun (from three to eight degrees difference in coordinates), self-realization will be a natural process, going along with physical growth. There will be no need for vain searching. This is the case for Marilyn Monroe (Figure 4) with Mercury Scout and for Audrey Hepburn (Figure 7) with Chiron Scout.

If a planet is very close to the Sun (less than three degrees) it is called combust. This planet is losing its energy and can't really be the real Scout. A person with this Scout might cease development at some stage or start going in circles. In the best-case scenario, with full awareness this person can be very independent.

Let's look more closely at the qualities of each planet when it plays the role of Doryphoros. Mercury and Venus play this role much more often than the other planets because they are inner planets. They are located between the Sun and the Earth and never stray far from the Sun in our charts.

The Moon

Our night luminary is very changeable, which is why a creative search and discovering one's identity will be inconsistent if the Moon is the first Oriental planet. This person will be sensitive, emotional and romantic. The Moon imparts amazing imagination and intuition. Such people may find themselves through music, poetry and art. The element of Water, as well as travelling, will be very important for them. They put all of their soul into the things that look meaningful. In the early years some of them might live in a fantasy world that is more important than reality. Parents should never discourage these kids from their fantasies. People with the Moon Scout have problems with restrictions; they need their freedom in addition to the understanding of others.

Mercury

With Mercury Scout people need contacts and information, which can come through talking to people, reading books and exploring the internet. In order to develop their creative nature these people have to be among others or at least have some other way of sharing information. The Scout Mercury gives them a curious and vivid mind.

In the vocational field, Mercury as a Scout brings abilities that are valuable for being a writer, scientist or merchant. If Mercury is in air or water signs, then occupations such as writer, journalist, translator and salesperson are on the top of the list. If Mercury Scout is in earth or fire signs, there might be a preference to work in the fields of business or science.

Venus

Individuals with Venus Scout really need a comfortable and beautiful environment for their harmonious personal development. Children with this Scout can't stand conflicts. People with Venus Doryphoros are good in manifesting themselves through art, dance, music and poetry. They have exceptional artistic taste and create beauty all around them. If you go to a dinner in their home, you will see a beautifully set table, the house decorated perfectly and the hostess's outfit flawlessly matched with accessories. People with this Scout can also be exceptional fashion designers and estheticians.

Do you recall that Mercury and Venus play the Scout role much more frequently than other planets? This means dividing people into two big groups: rational and sensual. And isn't that how it is generally happening in our world?

Mars

Creative searching and personal development are active and impulsive. This type needs challenges as well as freedom, and many of them become pioneers. Comfort is too boring for them. They have no patience. Mars Scout rushes ahead with great enthusiasm and excitement, sometimes realizing the meaning of their actions only much later. There are a lot of athletes, politicians and military people here.

Jupiter

Individuals with Jupiter Scout need authorities who they can trust and admire. It doesn't have to be a person; it could be just an idea that the individual will be deeply involved with. Generally these people are interested in ideology and philosophy. They want to make the world a better place. Jupiter Scout wants socializing, not for learning (like Mercury) but for manifesting ideas and opinions. These people need popularity because they crave recognition and approval from others.

This Scout can make a person a teacher, manager, priest, spiritual leader or politician.

It is important to give kids with Jupiter Scout the right kind of guidance, and the earlier the better; otherwise, it will be difficult to change their life views later. Kids also need to be taught to respect other people because they might have the tendency to overestimate their own importance.

Saturn

Saturn-Scout brings good analytical skills, stability and persistence in developing creative abilities. People with this Scout need discipline and their own space, often preferring to be alone. They don't need socializing; time to think without distractions is more important. These individuals are very careful in their conclusions.

Saturn as a Scout can bring an interest in philosophy. Having a firm system of priorities and personal goals really helps these people in finding their identity.

In the worst-case scenario, they might become too pessimistic, distant and gloomy. All of this happens because they clearly understand the imperfection of human beings and have no recipe to cure it. A couple of well-known philosophers had Saturn as a Scout: Baruch Spinoza, a Dutch philosopher from the seventeenth century, and Arthur Schopenhauer, a German philosopher of the early eighteen century. However, Spinoza had a combust Saturn, and Schopenhauer might have too, though we cannot be completely sure because his birth time is unknown.

Uranus

The personal development of individuals with the Uranus Scout is unpredictable. They might experience sudden enlightenment, which may shock other people. Full freedom is necessary for their self-realization. There is no discipline for those people. Nobody should put them in shackles. Could you imagine this in our society? There we have a problem: kids with the Uranus Scout should have freedom in expressing their spontaneous individuality and talents, but they also need to be taught to respect other people's plans and ways of thinking.

There might be people with supernatural abilities in this group (or great astrologers, or reformers). For example, Johannes Kepler, German mathematician, astronomer and astrologer, had Uranus as a Scout, as did Galileo Galilei (Uranus Scout was in a square aspect with the Sun in his chart, which probably brought problems in establishing his views).

Neptune

People with this Scout planet need love and faith; personal development isn't possible without them. These individuals can be daydreamers whose ideas are not understood by others. Their realization comes from mysticism, religion, music, art and poetry. Neptune doesn't make their self-development easy in our materialistic world. It is necessary for people with this Scout to find balance: follow their ideals but avoid illusions.

Pluto

The Pluto Scout requires extreme circumstances, chaos, challenges and tension for self-development. These individuals shouldn't be alone; they need crowds. In safe and calm environments they may be dull and boring, but they will become powerful and noticeable in extreme circumstances. They are ones who bring chaos to order. Times of crisis are the best for personal development of the Scout-Pluto people.

We can find people in risky occupations among them: surgeons, stunt men, investigators, firemen, as well as astrologers, prophets and those who work with the 'beyond' world. Michel Nostradamus was one of them.

Chiron

It is very unlikely that personal development with this Scout will be steady. Individuals with this Scout planet might go from one extreme to another. They will find their own truth by exploring opposite experiences, from trying alternatives. The Scout Chiron needs to always have choices. Even on one subject they might prefer having a couple of different teachers, ultimately choosing the one that is right for them. It is necessary for them to have objective information from different sides. A certain amount of inconsistency is just the way of their self-development.

Proserpina

People with Proserpina Scout also should have a variety of everything. Being a planet of transformation, Proserpina allows one to have complete charge over one's life and personality. She plays a Scout role rarely; mostly for Libras and Scorpios (because this planet is very slow and for two generations is located in the mentioned signs).

Practical skills (the more the better) are vital for these individuals. They can become scattered but will eventually find their system. Even small things in their lives can lead to big changes. These people can be excellent jewelers, scientists, restorers and doctors.

Conclusion

I sincerely hope that this book might provide you with some useful tools for personal discovery. I am aware that the search for true identity can take a lifetime. My own spiritual journey will never end, and that is okay.

Usually our personal growth doesn't follow a straight line; it is more of a spiral. We sometimes rediscover some slightly forgotten things from a different perspective. If we don't like something in our character, it is pointless to blame our astrological charts and do nothing: "Well, it is written in the stars. What can I do?" Actually, we can do a lot to improve ourselves...or we can just truly accept ourselves the way we are. Those two choices are equal.

Sometimes seeing an explanation about why some of our traits are present can be all we need in order to accept them. Acceptance (of any kind) always makes life easier. The same can be said about the charts and the characters of the people in our lives. Understanding is one of the main keys in harmonious relationships (after Love, of course).

I wish you a happy journey towards yourself and many interesting discoveries.

Namaste.

Bibliography

Globa, Pavel. Lunar Astrology. Moscow, Russia. 1996.

Globa, Pavel. Lectures. Moscow, Russia. 1985 – 1987.

C.G.Jung. Psychology of the Unconscious. Mineola, NY: Dover Publications, 2014

Lomakina, Olga. Planetary Psychoanalysis. Moscow, Russia: Center of Cosmology, 2000

Massey, Anne. Venus. Woodbury, MN: Llewellyn Publications, 2006

Appendix

Ephemeris of Proserpina

Proserpina in Libra

1935

January	7:44:59R	May	7:18:38	September	7:52:01
February	7:38:12	June	7:20:19D	October	8:04:02
March	7:29:40	July	7:27:30	November	8:12:19
April	7:22:16	August	7:38:52	December	8:15:17

1936

January	8:12:45R	May	7:46:20	September	8:19:30
February	8:06:01	June	7:47:56D	October	8:31:33
March	7:57:29	July	7:55:02	November	8:39:55
April	7:50:03	August	8:06:22	December	8:42:58

1937

January	8:40:31R	May	8:14:02	September	8:46:59
February	8:33:49	June	8:15:33D	October	8:59:04
March	8:25:17	July	8:22:34	November	9:07:30
April	8:17:49	August	8:33:51	December	9:10:38

1938

January	9:08:16R	May	8:41:44	September	9:14:28
February	9:01:37	June	8:43:10D	October	9:26:35
March	8:53:06	July	8:50:06	November	9:35:06
April	8:45:36	August	9:01:20	December	9:38:18

1939

January	9:36:01R	May	9:09:27	September	9:47:57
February	9:29:26	June	9:10:47D	October	9:54:06
March	9:20:55	July	9:17:39	November	10:02:41
April	9:13:23	August	9:28:50	December	10:06:00

Proserpina in Libra continued:

1940

January	10:03:47R	May	9:37:09	September	10:09:25
February	9:57:14	June	9:38:24D	October	10:21:37
March	9:48:44	July	9:45:11	November	10:30:16
April	9:41:09	August	9:56:19	December	10:33:40

1941

January	10:31:32R	May	10:04:51	September	10:36:54
February	10:23:03	June	10:06:01D	October	10:49:08
March	10:16:33	July	10:12:44	November	10:57:52
April	10:08:56	August	10:23:48	December	11:01:21

1942

January	10:59:17R	May	10:32:34	September	11:04:23
February	10:52:51	June	10:33:38D	October	11:16:39
March	10:44:22	July	10:40:16	November	11:25:27
April	10:36:43	August	10:51:18	December	11:29:01

1943

January	11:27:03R	May	11:00:17	September	11:31:52
February	11:20:39	June	11:01:16D	October	11:44:10
March	11:12:11	July	11:07:49	November	11:53:02
April	11:04:30	August	11:18:47	December	11:56:41

1944

January	11:54:48R	May	11:27:59	September	11:59:21
February	11:48:28	June	11:28:53D	October	12:11:41
March	11:40:00	July	11L35:21	November	12:20:37
April	11:32:17	August	11:46:17	December	12:24:22

Proserpina in Libra continued:

1945

January	12:22:33R	May	11:55:42	September	12:26:50
February	12:16:16	June	11:56:31D	October	12:39:12
March	12:07:49	July	12:02:54	November	12:48:12
April	12:00:04	August	12:13:46	December	12:52:02

1946

January	12:50:18R	May	12:23:25	September	12:54:18
February	12:44:04	June	12:24:09D	October	13:06:43
March	12:35:37	July	12:30:27	November	13:15:47
April	12:27:51	August	12:41:16	December	13:19:42

1947

January	13:18:03R	May	12:51:08	September	13:21:47
February	13:11:52	June	12:51:46D	October	13:34:13
March	13:03:26	July	12:58:00	November	13:43:21
April	12:55:38	August	13:08:45	December	13:47:22

1948

January	13:45:48R	May	13:18:51	September	13:49:16
February	13:39:40	June	13:19:24D	October	14:01:44
March	13:31:15	July	13:25:33	November	14:10:56
April	13:23:25	August	13:36:15	December	14:15:02

1949

January	14:13:32R	May	13:46:34	September	14:16:45
February	14:07:28	June	13:47:02D	October	14:29:15
March	13:59:04	July	13:53:06	November	14:38:31
April	13:51:12	August	14:03:45	December	14:42:41

Proserpina in Libra continued:

1950

January	14:41:17R	May	14:14:17	September	14:44:14
February	14:35:17	June	14:14:40D	October	14:56:45
March	14:26:53	July	14:20:39	November	15:06:05
April	14:18:59	August	14:31:14	December	15:10:21

1951

January	15:09:02R	May	14:42:00	September	15:11:42
February	15:03:05	June	14:42:18D	October	15:24:16
March	14:54:42	July	14:48:12	November	15:33:40
April	14:46:46	August	14:58:44	December	15:38:01

1952

January	15:26:46R	May	15:09:44	September	15:39:11
February	15:30:53	June	15:09:56D	October	15:51:46
March	15:22:31	July	15:15:45	November	16:01:14
April	15:14:33	August	15:26:14	December	16:15:40

1953

January	16:04:31R	May	15:27:37	September	16:06:40
February	15:58:41	June	15:37:35D	October	16:19:17
March	15:50:20	July	15:43:18	November	16:28:49
April	15:42:21	August	15:53:44	December	16:33:20

1954

January	16:32:15R	May	16:05:10	September	16:34:09
February	16:26:28	June	16:05:13D	October	16:46:17
March	16:18:09	July	16:10:52	November	16:56:33
April	16:10:08	August	16:21:13	December	17:00:59

Proserpina in Libra continued:

1955

January	17:00:00R	May	16:32:54	September	17:01:37
February	16:54:16	June	16:32:51D	October	17:14:17
March	16:45:58	July	16:38:25	November	17:23:57
April	16:37:55	August	16:48:43	December	17:28:39

1956

January	17:27:44R	May	17:00:38	September	17:29:06
February	17:22:04	June	17:00:30D	October	17:41:48
March	17:13:47	July	17:05:59	November	17:51:31
April	17:05:43	August	17:16:13	December	17:56:18

1957

January	17:55:28R	May	17:28:21	September	17:56:35
February	17:49:52	June	17:28:08D	October	18:09:18
March	17:41:36	July	17:33:32	November	18:19:05
April	17:33:30	August	17:43:43	December	18:23:57

1958

January	18:23:13R	May	17:56:05	September	18:24:04
February	18:17:40	June	17:55:47D	October	18:36:48
March	18:09:25	July	18:01:06	November	18:46:39
April	18:01:18	August	18:11:13	December	18:51:36

1959

January	18:50:56R	May	18:23:49	September	18:51:32
February	18:45:28	June	18:23:26D	October	19:04:18
March	18:37:14	July	18:28:40	November	19:14:13
April	18:29:06	August	18:38:43	December	19:19:15

Proserpina in Libra continued:

1960

January	19:18:41R	May	18:51:33	September	19:19:01
February	19:13:15	June	18:51:05D	October	19:31:48
March	19:05:03	July	18:56:13	November	19:41:47
April	18:56:53	August	10:06:13	December	19:46:54

1961

January	19:46:25R	May	19:19:17	September	19:46:30
February	19:41:03	June	19:18:43D	October	19:59:19
March	19:32:52	July	19:23:47	November	20:09:21
April	19:24:41	August	19:33:43	December	20:14:33

1962

January	20:14:08R	May	19:47:01	September	20:13:59
February	20:08:51	June	19:26:42D	October	20:26:49
March	20:00:41	July	19:51:21	November	20:36:55
April	19:52:28	August	20:01:14	December	20:42:12

1963

January	20:41:52R	May	20:14:45	September	20:41:27
February	20:36:38	June	20:14:01D	October	20:54:19
March	20:28:30	July	20:18:55	November	21:04:28
April	20:20:16	August	20:28:44	December	21:09:50

1964

January	21:09:36R	May	20:42:29	September	21:08:56
February	21:04:26	June	20:41:41D	October	21:21:49
March	20:56:19	July	20:46:29	November	21:30:02
April	20:48:04	August	20:56:14	December	21:37:29

Proserpina in Libra continued:

1965

January	21:37:20R	May	21:10:13	September	21:36:25
February	21:32:13	June	21:09:20D	October	21:49:19
March	21:24:08	July	21:14:03	November	21:59:35
April	21:15:52	August	21:23:44	December	22:05:07

1966

January	22:05:03R	May	21:37:57	September	22:03:54
February	22:00:01	June	21:36:59D	October	22:16:48
March	21:51:57	July	21:41:37	November	22:27:09
April	21:43:40	August	21:51:15	December	22:32:46

1967

January	22:32:47R	May	22:05:42	September	22:31:22
February	22:27:48	June	22:04:38D	October	22:44:18
March	22:19:46	July	22:09:12	November	22:54:42
April	22:11:28	August	22:18:45	December	23:00:24

1968

January	23:00:30R	May	22:33:26	September	22:58:51
February	22:55:36	June	22:32:18D	October	23:11:48
March	22:47:35	July	22:36:46	November	23:22:15
April	22:39:16	August	22:46:15	December	23:28:02

1969

January	23:28:14R	May	23:01:11	September	23:26:20
February	23;23:23	June	22:59:57D	October	23:39:18
March	23:15:24	July	23:04:20	November	23:49:49
April	23:07:03	August	23:13:46	December	23:55:41

Proserpina in Libra continued:

1970

January	23:55:57R	May	23:28:55	September	23:53:49
February	23:51:10	June	23:27:37D	October	24:06:48
March	23:43:13	July	23:31:55	November	24:17:22
April	23:34:51	August	23:41:16	December	24:23:19

1971

January	24:23:40R	May	23:56:40	September	24:21:17
February	24:18:57	June	23:55:17D	October	24:34:17
March	24:11:02	July	23:59:29	November	24:44:55
April	24:02:40	August	24:08:47	December	24:50:57

1972

January	24:51:23R	May	24:24:25	September	24:48:46
February	24:46:45	June	24:22:57D	October	25:01:47
March	24:38:51	July	24:27:04	November	25:12:28
April	24:30:28	August	24:36:17	December	25:18:25

1973

January	25:19:07R	May	24:52:09	September	25:16:15
February	25:14:32	June	24:50:36D	October	25:29:17
March	25:06:40	July	24:54:39	November	25:40:01
April	24:58:16	August	25:03:48	December	25:46:12

1974

January	25:46:50R	May	25:19:54	September	25:43:44
February	25:42:19	June	25:18:16D	October	25:56:46
March	25:34:29	July	25:22:13	November	26:07:34
April	25:26:40	August	25:31:19	December	26:13:15

Proserpina in Libra continued:

1975

January	26:14:33R	May	25:47:39	September	26:11:13
February	26:10:06	June	25:45:56D	October	26:24:16
March	26:02:18	July	25:49:48	November	26:35:07
April	25:53:52	August	25:58:50	December	26:41:28

1976

January	26:42:15R	May	26:15:24	September	26:38:40
February	26:37:53	June	26:13:37D	October	26:15:45
March	26:30:07	July	26:17:23	November	27:02:39
April	26:21:40	August	26:26:20	December	27:09:06

1977

January	27:09:58R	May	26:43:09	September	27:06:10
February	27:05:40	June	26:41:17D	October	27:19:15
March	26:57:56	July	26:44:58	November	27:30:12
April	26:49:28	August	26:53:51	December	27:36:43

1978

January	27:37:41R	May	27:10:54	September	27:33:39
February	27:33:27	June	27:08:57D	October	27:46:44
March	27:25:45	July	27:12:33	November	27:57:45
April	27:17:17	August	27:21:22	December	28:04:21

1979

January	28:05:24R	May	27:38:39	September	28:01:08
February	28:01:13	June	27:36:37D	October	28:14:14
March	27:53:34	July	27:40:08	November	28:25:17
April	27:45:05	August	27:48:53	December	28:31:58

Proserpina in Libra continued:

1980

January	28:33:06R	May	28:06:25	September	28:28:37
February	28:29:00	June	28:04:18D	October	28:41:43
March	28:21:23	July	28:07:44	November	28:52:50
April	28:12:53	August	28:16:24	December	28:59:35

1981

January	29:00:49	May	28:34:40	September	28:56:06
February	28:56:47	June	28:31:58D	October	29:09:13
March	28:49:12	July	28:35:19	November	29:20:22
April	28:40:42	August	28:43:55	December	29:27:12

1982

January	29:28:31R	May	29:01:55	September	29:23:35
February	29:24:34	June	28:59:39D	October	29:36:42
March	29:17:01	July	29:02:54	November	29:47:55
April	29:08:30	August	29:11:26	December	29:54:50

1983

January	29:56:13R	May	29:29:41	September	29:51:04
February	29:52:20	June	29:27:20D	October	0:04:11 *Scorp*
March	29:44:50	July	29:30:30	November	0:15:27
April	29:36:18	August	29:38:57	December	0:22:27

Proserpina in Scorpio 1984

January	0:23:56R	May	29:57:26 **Lib**	September	0:18:32
February	0:20:07	June	29:55:00D	October	0:31:41
March	0:12:38	July	29:58:05	November	0:42:59
April	0:04:07	August	0:06:28 **Scorp**	December	0:50:04

Proserpina in Libra continued:

1985

January	0:51:38R	May	0:25:12	September	0:46:01
February	0:47:53	June	0:22:41D	October	0:59:10
March	0:40:27	July	0:25:41	November	1:10:31
April	0:31:55	August	0:34:00	December	1:17:40

1986

January	1:19:20R	May	0:52:57	September	1:13:30
February	1:15:40	June	0:50:22D	October	1:26:29
March	1:08:16	July	0:53:16	November	1:38:03
April	0:59:44	August	1:01:31	December	1:45:17

1987

January	1:47:02R	May	1:20:43	September	1:40:59
February	1:43:26	June	1:18:03D	October	1:54:08
March	1:36:05	July	1:20:52	November	1:05:36
April	1:37:32	August	1:29:02	December	2:12:54

1988

January	2:14:44R	May	1:48:29	September	2:08:28
February	2:11:13	June	1:45:44	October	2:21:38
March	2:03:54	July	12:48:28D	November	2:33:08
April	1:55:21	August	1:56:34	December	2:40:31

1989

January	2:42:26R	May	2:16:14	September	2:35:57
February	2:38:59	June	2:13:25	October	2:49:07
March	2:31:42	July	2:16:04D	November	3:00:39
April	2:23:10	August	2:24:05	December	3:08:07

Proserpina in Libra continued:

1990

January	3:10:08R	May	2:44:00	September	3:03:26
February	3:06:45	June	2:41:06	October	3:16:36
March	2:59:31	July	2:43:40D	November	3:28:11
April	2:50:58	August	2:51:37	December	3:35:44

1991

January	3:37:49R	May	3:11:46	September	3:30:55
February	3:34:33	June	3:08:48	October	3:44:05
March	3:27:20	July	3:11:16D	November	3:55:43
April	3:18:47	August	3:19:08	December	4:03:20

1992

January	4:05:31R	May	3:39:32	September	3:58:24
February	4:02:18	June	3:36:29	October	4:11:34
March	3:55:09	July	3:38:52D	November	4:23:15
April	3:36:35	August	3:46:40	December	4:30:57

1993

January	4:33:13R	May	4:07:18	September	4:25:53
February	4:30:04	June	4:04:11	October	4:39:03
March	4:22:57	July	4:06:28D	November	4:50:47
April	4:14:24	August	4:14:12	December	4:58:33

1994

January	5:00:54R	May	4:35:04	September	4:53:23
February	4:57:50	June	4:31:52	October	5:06:32
March	4:50:46	July	4:34:05D	November	5:18:18
April	4:42:13	August	4:41:43	December	5:26:09

Proserpina in Scorpio continued:

1995

January	5:28:35R	May	5:02:50	September	5:20:52
February	5:25:36	June	4:59:34	October	5:34:01
March	5:18:35	July	5:01:41	November	5:45:50
April	5:10:01	August	5:09:15	December	5:53:45

1996

January	5:56:17R	May	5:30:37	September	5:48:21
February	5:53:22	June	5:27:16	October	6:01:30
March	5:46:23	July	5:29:18D	November	6:13:21
April	5:37:50	August	5:36:47	December	6:21:21

1997

January	6:23:58R	May	5:58:23	September	6:15:50
February	6:21:08	June	5:54:57	October	6:28:59
March	6:14:12	July	5:26:54D	November	6:40:53
April	6:05:39	August	6:04:19	December	6:48:57

1998

January	6:51:39R	May	6:26:09	September	6:43:19
February	6:48:53	June	6:22:39	October	6:56:28
March	6:42:00	July	6:24:31D	November	7:08:24
April	6:33:28	August	6:31:51	December	7:16:33

1999

January	7:19:20	May	6:53:56	September	7:10:48
February	7:16:39R	June	6:50:21	October	7:23:57
March	7:09:49	July	6:52:07D	November	7:35:56
April	7:01:16	August	6:59:23	December	7:44:09

Proserpina in Scorpio continued:

2000

January	7:47:01	May	7:21:42	September	7:38:18
February	7:44:25R	June	7:19:03	October	7:51:26
March	7:37:37	July	7:19:44D	November	8:03:27
April	7:29:05	August	7:26:55	December	8:11:44

2001

January	8:14:42	May	7:49:28	September	8:05:47
February	8:12:10R	June	7:45:45	October	8:18:55
March	8:05:26	July	7:47:21D	November	8:30:58
April	7:56:54	August	7:54:27	December	8:39:20

2002

January	8:42:23	May	8:17:15	September	8:33:16
February	8:39:56R	June	8:13:27	October	8:46:24
March	8:33:14	July	8:14:58D	November	8:58:20
April	8:24:43	August	8:22:00	December	9:06:56

2003

January	9:10:04	May	8:45:01	September	9:00:46
February	9:07:41R	June	8:41:10	October	9:13:53
March	9:01:03	July	8:42:35D	November	9:26:01
April	8:52:32	August	8:49:32	December	9:34:31

2004

January	9:37:45	May	9:12:48	September	9:28:15
February	9:35:27R	June	9:08:52	October	9:41:22
March	9:28:51	July	9:01:12D	November	9:53:32
April	9:20:21	August	9:17:04	December	10:02:06

Proserpina in Scorpio continued:

2005

January	10:05:25	May	9:40:35	September	9:55:44
February	10:03:12R	June	9:36:34	October	10:08:51
March	9:56:40	July	9:37:49D	November	10:21:03
April	9:48:09	August	9:44:37	December	10:29:43

2006

January	10:33:06	May	10:08:22	September	10:23:14
February	10:30:58R	June	10:04:17	October	10:36:20
March	10:24:28	July	10:05:27D	November	10:48:34
April	10:15:58	August	10:12:09	December	10:57:17

2007

January	11:00:46	May	10:36:08	September	10:50:43
February	10:58:43R	June	10:31:59	October	11:03:49
March	10:52:16	July	10:33:04D	November	11:16:05
April	10:43:47	August	10:38:42	December	11:24:52

2008

January	11:28:37	May	11:03:55	September	11:18:13
February	11:26:28R	June	10:59:42	October	11:31:17
March	11:20:05	July	11:00:41D	November	11:43:36
April	11:11:36	August	11:07:14	December	11:52:27

2009

January	11:56:07	May	11:31:42	September	11:45:52
February	11:54:13R	June	11:27:25	October	11:58:46
March	11:47:53	July	11:28:19D	November	12:11:07
April	11:39:25	August	11:34:47	December	12:20:02

Proserpina in Scorpio continued:

2010

January	12:23:47	May	11:59:29	September	12:13:12
February	12:21:58R	June	11:55:08	October	12:26:15
March	12:15:41	July	11:55:56D	November	12:38:37
April	12:07:14	August	12:02:20	December	12:47:37

2011

January	12:51:27	May	12:27:16	September	12:40:41
February	12:49:43R	June	12:22:50	October	12:53:44
March	12:43:29	July	12:23:34D	November	13:06:08
April	12:35:03	August	12:29:52	December	13:15:12

2012

January	13:19:07	May	12:55:03	September	13:08:11
February	13:17:28R	June	12:50:33	October	13:21:13
March	13:11:18	July	12:51:12D	November	13:33:29
April	13:02:52	August	12:57:25	December	13:42:47

2013

January	12:46:47	May	13:22:50	September	13:35:40
February	13:45:13R	June	13:18:16	October	13:48:41
March	13:39:06	July	13:18:50D	November	14:01:10
April	13:30:41	August	13:24:58	December	14:10:22

2014

January	14:14:27	May	13:50:37	September	14:03:10
February	14:12:58R	June	14:45:59	October	14:16:10
March	14:06:54	July	13:46:28D	November	14:28:40
April	13:58:30	August	13:52:31	December	14:37:56

Proserpina in Scorpio continued:

2015

January	14:42:07	May	14:18:24	September	14:30:40
February	14:40:42R	June	14:13:43	October	14:43:39
March	14:34:42	July	14:14:06D	November	14:56:11
April	14:26:19	August	14:20:04	December	15:05:31

2016

January	15:09:47	May	14:46:12	September	14:58:10
February	15:08:27R	June	14:41:26	October	15:11:08
March	15:02:30	July	14:41:44D	November	15:23:41
April	14:54:08	August	14:47:37	December	15:33:05

2017

January	15:37:26	May	15:13:59	September	15:25:39
February	15:36:12R	June	15:09:09	October	15:38:37
March	15:30:18	July	15:09:22D	November	15:51:12
April	15:21:57	August	15:15:11	December	16:00:40

2018

January	16:05:06	May	15:41:46	September	15:53:09
February	16:03:56R	June	15:36:52	October	16:06:05
March	15:58:06	July	15:37:00D	November	16:18:42
April	15:49:46	August	15:42:44	December	16:28:14

2019

January	16:23:45	May	16:09:34	September	16:20:39
February	16:31:41R	June	16:04:36	October	16:33:34
March	16:25:54	July	16:04:38D	November	16:46:13
April	16:17:35	August	16:10:17	December	16:45:38

Proserpina in Scorpio continued:

2020

January	17:00:25	May	16:37:21	September	16:48:09
February	16:59:25R	June	16:32:19	October	17:01:03
March	16:53:42	July	16:32:17D	November	17:13:43
April	16:45:21	August	16:37:51	December	17:23:23

2021

January	17:28:04	May	17:05:08	September	17:15:39
February	17:27:09R	June	17:00:03	October	17:28:32
March	17:21:30	July	16:59:53D	November	17:41:13
April	17:13:13	August	17:05:24	December	17:50:57

2022

January	17:55:43	May	17:32:56	September	17:43:09
February	17:54:54R	June	17:27:47	October	17:56:00
March	17:49:18	July	17:27:34D	November	18:08:43
April	17:41:02	August	17:32:58	December	18:18:31